FAVORITE RECIPES of the SOUTH

FAVORITE RECIPES
of the
SOUTH

PORTLAND HOUSE

CONTENTS

Introduced and Edited by Nina Morgan
Designed by Philip Clucas
Coordinated by Hanni Penrose
Photographed by Jean-Paul Paireault
Produced by Ted Smart, David Gibbon and
Gerald Hughes

CLB 1614
© 1988 Colour Library Books Ltd., Guildford, Surrey, England.
All rights reserved.
Text filmsetting by Words and Spaces, Hampshire, England.
Printed and bound in Hong Kong.
Published in 1988 by Portland House, a division of dilithium Press, Ltd.,
distributed by Crown Publishers, Inc.,
225 Park Avenue South, New York, New York 10003
ISBN 0 517 61392 1
h g f e d c b a

INTRODUCTION

The very mention of southern food evokes visions of famed southern hospitality. And, of course, no small ingredient of this hospitality is southern food. Although the southern states are often grouped as a geographic entity, they are, in fact, very diverse. Their different characteristics are strongly represented in their cuisine. When you see crisp southern fried chicken, hot biscuits, blackeyed peas, cornmeal mush and boiled turnip greens on the menu, you know you must be in Dixie. But when you taste a spicy crawfish boil or indulge in a gumbo, you could only be in Louisiana. The taste of fresh peach pie brings you home to Georgia, while the creamy richness of she-crab soup calls to mind the gracious, wide verandas of old Charleston.

Contrasts in geography and history are responsible for this diversity. The region stretches from the flat coastal plains of the Atlantic to the rolling hills of the Piedmont and into the rugged and beautiful reaches of the Appalachian Mountains. To the west, cotton was king, and Old Man River, the mighty Mississippi, was both the lifeline to the outer world and the source of delicious freshwater fish which were transformed into delectable dishes in the kitchens throughout the region.

Settlement of some parts of the South began very early and each group of settlers left behind their favorite recipes. The Spanish explored Florida as far back as 1560, yet some of their influence remains in the Florida version of the Spanish dish paella, still served with pride in the Governor's Mansion in Tallahassee today. The English were the dominant settlers along the Atlantic coast in Virginia and Georgia, and their influence is still to be seen in the menus there today. French settlers spread their culinary heritage far and wide, especially in Louisiana, Mississippi, and the Carolinas.

The various immigrant groups who came to the South in search of religious freedom also brought their favorite recipes with them to add to the culinary melange. The French Huguenot tradition is prominent in South Carolina, and the tradition of simple and delicious cooking so characteristic of the Shakers is evident around their settlements in Kentucky.

Wherever you travel in the South you are sure to find biscuits. Recipes for biscuits are generally vague. What is the secret to this most southern of foods? Now, as in the early days, biscuits are popular because they are fast and easy to make. The basic recipes are simple, but there is more to biscuit making than meets the eye, and this is a skill best learned at your southern grandmother's knee. Although there are some basic methods, it is best to keep in mind that where light, fluffy biscuits are concerned "rules can no more make a cook than sermons make a saint."

You can be sure that wherever you travel in the South you will taste the result of the traditional gracious southern hospitality. The diverse cuisine reflects the pride of place and respect for the past that are an inseparable part of life here. If you have never visited the southern states, this collection of recipes, gathered from good cooks throughout the region, will certainly whet your appetite. If you already know the area, these recipes will bring back happy memories.

FLORIDA

Florida, which takes its name from the Spanish *Pascua Florida*, the Easter feast of flowers, has had a varied history. Early French and Spanish explorers competed in the sixteenth century to establish settlements in its northeastern corner, and these outposts represent some of the oldest in North America. The beautiful and historic city of St. Augustine, on the Atlantic coast, which celebrated its 400th anniversary in 1964, is the oldest in the United States. Florida's history is unusual and interesting. Initially under the control of the Spanish, she became a short-lived, independent republic before being briefly annexed to Mexico. Under political pressure, the United States took over the peninsula and held it in trust for Spain, and it was not until 1845 that Florida finally joined the Union.

When they think of Florida most people think of the miles of beautiful white beaches along the Atlantic and Gulf coasts which have made Florida America's vacation land. Vacationers come to Florida to enjoy the beaches, and many well-to-do northerners and retirees have migrated permanently to the communities around Miami. There is another side to Florida, too. The flat, swampy, but subtly beautiful wilderness which makes up the Everglades in the southern part of the state has its origin in a long series of lakes and streams that begins halfway up the interior in the low hills of the central ridge. The atmosphere of the Old South still survives in the eastern part of the state, especially in the rolling hills around Tallahassee, the state capital. In contrast to much of Florida, cotton was king here, and wealthy planters built beautiful mansions set in romantic landscapes of giant oaks draped in trailing Spanish moss.

This southern heritage is reflected in the survival of such traditional southern fare as collard green soup and corn bread still served in the kitchens of the Governor's Mansion in Tallahassee. The Spanish have also left their mark on Florida cuisine, and this has been greatly reinforced by large communities of Cuban immigrants who have settled in the state. Typically Latin dishes such as paella, a wonderful rice-based seafood and meat dish named for the two-handled iron frying pan in which it is traditionally served, are given an extra boost with a full dose of fresh Florida seafood. Flan, a Mexican and Spanish dessert similar to baked custard, flavored with caramelized sugar, is another favorite.

But the greatest culinary inspiration in a state also known for its vast production of citrus fruits and vegetables, is undoubtedly fresh fish and seafood. Some of the favorite seafood ingredients are common only in Florida. Stone crabs, unique to the Florida area, are harvested for their exceptionally large claws, and the succulent meat is served in many different ways. The local lobster is the rock lobster, which may lack the large claws of the northern species but lacks nothing in flavor. Appalochicola, on the Gulf coast, supports a local oyster, shrimp, and seafood industry which provides the delicious Appalochicola oysters favored by many Florida cooks. The warm coastal waters are a source of many varieties of fish including snapper, dolphin, and tile fish, which form the basis of many delicious meals. The Florida Keys, the string of sandy islands extending westwards off the southern tip of Florida, are a seafood lover's paradise. Conch shells, which are so common in the Keys that the natives even hold conch shell blowing contests, provide an unusual taste-treat which can be prepared by marinating rather than cooking.

The inland waters, too, make their contribution. Lake Okeechobee, set at the northern edge of the Everglades, and the second largest body of fresh water wholly in the United States, is known for its catfish, a popular food in many forms. The swamps of the Everglades are the source of frog legs, a much prized delicacy.

This collection of recipes, gathered in Palm Beach and Tallahassee, illustrates the wide variety of Florida's cuisine. Florida may be the place "where the sun spends the winter," but for inventive seafood cooks, it is certainly the place where they would like to spend all of their time!

Facing page: Florida Deviled Blue Crab.

COLLARD GREEN SOUP

These simple ingredients blend together to make a wonderful soup.

Preparation Time: 30 minutes
Cooking Time: 4 hours
Serves: 10

INGREDIENTS

2 ham hocks
2 quarts water
1 cup Great Northern Beans, soaked overnight and drained
1lb Chorizo sausage
1lb white bacon, diced
1 large onion, chopped
1 clove garlic, minced
12oz frozen, chopped collard greens
Salt and pepper to taste

METHOD

Boil the ham hocks in the water for 1 hour. Add the soaked beans to the soup and simmer until tender, about 2 hours. Meanwhile, sauté the sausage, drain and set aside. Clean the frying pan, then sauté the bacon until crisp. Remove and set aside, then fry the garlic and onion in the bacon drippings. When the beans are nearly cooked, add the sautéed bacon, sausage, onion and garlic to the pot. Cook the collard greens in a small amount of boiling water for 15 minutes, or follow the directions on the package. Add to the soup and season to taste with salt and pepper. Simmer for 45 minutes to allow the flavors to blend.

GOVERNOR'S MANSION,
TALLAHASSEE, FL

SHRIMP AND MUSHROOM SALAD

This original salad makes use of some of Florida's most delicious seafood.

Collard Green Soup (top), Flan (bottom left), Shrimp and Mushroom Salad (bottom center) and Wild Duck Breasts with Raspberries (bottom right).

Preparation Time: 30 minutes
Cooking Time: 1 minute
Serves: 8

INGREDIENTS

2lbs cooked shrimp
½lb snow peas, topped and tailed
1lb very white mushrooms, sliced
1 cup toasted pecans
2 heads Boston or bibb lettuce

VINAIGRETTE

1 tbsp Dijon-style mustard
1 clove garlic, minced
4 tbsps cider vinegar
Dash lime juice
1 cup salad oil
Salt and pepper to taste

METHOD

Peel and devein the shrimp. Blanch the snow peas in the boiling salted water for 45 seconds, then drain. Toss together the mushrooms, shrimp, snow peas and pecans. To prepare the vinaigrette, place the mustard, garlic, lime juice and vinegar in the bowl of a food processor. Pulse a few times, then run continuously while adding the oil in a slow stream. Season with salt and pepper to taste. To serve, toss the salad in the vinaigrette. Line salad plates with the lettuce and arrange the salad on top.

ART SMITH, GOVERNOR'S MANSION,
TALLAHASSEE, FL

WILD DUCK BREASTS WITH RASPBERRIES

Preparation Time: 30 minutes
Cooking Time: 35 minutes
Serves: 4

INGREDIENTS

4 wild duck breasts
Clarified butter for browning
Salt and pepper to taste

RASPBERRY SAUCE

1 pint raspberries
½ cup water
½ cup sugar
1 cup orange juice
Grated zest of 1 orange

GARNISH

Fresh raspberries
Fresh mint leaves

METHOD

First prepare the raspberry sauce by combining the raspberries, water, sugar and orange juice in a saucepan. Simmer the ingredients slowly for 20-25 minutes. Strain the sauce through a fine mesh sieve, then stir in the zest. Set aside while you roast the duck breasts. To prepare the duck, heat some clarified butter in a frying pan and place the duck, skin side down, in the hot pan. Carefully brown the skin. Remove the breasts to a roasting pan and roast on a rack for 10 to 15 minutes. Be careful not to overcook, roast only until the meat is light pink. Towards the end of the cooking time, spoon some of the raspberry sauce over the meat.

To serve, place several spoonfuls of the sauce onto each plate. Slice the meat diagonally and arrange on top of the sauce. Garnish with fresh raspberries and sprigs of mint.

For a very elegant dinner party, accompany this dish with "carved" vegetables. If you don't possess the skill, fresh, lightly cooked vegetables are also good.

GOVERNOR'S MANSION,
TALLAHASSEE, FL

KEY LIME PIE

Here is a recipe for the famous dessert from the Keys. It is delightfully sharp and refreshing.

Preparation Time: 30 minutes
Cooking Time: 25 minutes
Yield: 1 9-inch pie

Facing page: Key Lime Pie.

Above: Paella.

INGREDIENTS

GRAHAM CRACKER CRUST
1½ cups graham cracker crumbs
½ cup sugar
½ cup butter or margarine, melted

FILLING
2 eggs
15oz sweetened condensed milk
½ cup Key Lime juice
¼ tsp salt

TOPPING
1 cup sour cream
⅓ cup sugar
⅛ tsp salt

GARNISH
Graham cracker crumbs
Grated lime rind

METHOD

First prepare the crust by blending together the crust ingredients. Press the mixture firmly into a 9-inch pie plate. Bake at 350°F for 10 minutes. To prepare the filling, beat the eggs and milk together. Add the lime juice and salt. Pour the filling into the prepared crust and bake at 350°F for 10 minutes, or until set. Meanwhile, prepare the topping by combining the sour cream, sugar and salt. When the filling has set, spread this topping over the pie. Bake at 425°F for 5 minutes to allow the topping to set. Garnish the pie with graham cracker crumbs and grated lime rind before serving. Serve cold.

LIZ WILLIAMS, GOVERNOR'S MANSION, TALLAHASSEE, FL

FLAN

Serve this Spanish-inspired dessert with a fruit garnish of your choice.

Preparation Time: 20 minutes
Cooking Time: 45 minutes
Serves: 6

INGREDIENTS

1 cup plus 3 tbsps sugar
1 cup milk
1 cup light cream
4 eggs
4 egg yolks
1 tsp vanilla
Pinch cinnamon, nutmeg and ground cloves

METHOD

Place one cup of the sugar in a heavy skillet and cook over a high heat, stirring constantly, until the sugar becomes brown and syrupy − it will smoke slightly when it is nearly ready. Use this syrup to coat the bottom and sides of a 6-cup baking dish. Scald the milk and cream. In a separate bowl wisk together the eggs, yolks, remaining sugar and vanilla. Beat in a little of the hot milk first to stablize the mixture, then stir in the rest of the hot milk. Strain into the coated baking dish. Place the dish in a pan filled with boiling water and bake at 325°F for 45 minutes, or until a knife inserted in the center comes out clean.

GOVERNOR'S MANSION,
TALLAHASSEE, FL

PAELLA

Florida's Spanish heritage is well reflected in this version of a classic Spanish dish.

Preparation Time: 30 minutes
Cooking Time: 35 minutes
Serves: 8-10

INGREDIENTS

2 tbsps olive oil
2 tbsps butter
1 large onion, chopped
1 green pepper, chopped
2 cloves garlic, minced
1 chicken, cut into serving pieces
1lb smoked sausage, cut into 1-inch-thick slices
12oz yellow rice
3 cups stock or water
Salt to taste
2lbs shrimp, peeled and deveined
1lb clams, mussels or lobster (optional)
10oz tiny peas

METHOD

In a paella pan, sauté the onion, green pepper and garlic in a mixture of olive oil and the butter until limp. Remove the vegetables from the pan and set aside. Sauté the chicken pieces and sausage and set aside. Drain the pan, then return the vegetables and meat. Stir in the rice and liquid. Cover the pan with foil and place it in a 350°F oven. Bake for approximately 25 minutes. About ten minutes before the cooking time is up, stir in the seafood and the peas. Continue cooking until the rice is tender and the seafood is cooked but not over done.

GOVERNOR'S MANSION,
TALLAHASSEE, FL

FRIED SOFTSHELL BLUE CRAB

Blue crabs are common all over Florida, and fried softshell crabs are a typical Florida dish.

Preparation Time: 30 minutes
Cooking Time: 10-15 minutes
Serves: 4

INGREDIENTS

4 softshell blue crabs
1 egg, beaten
1 cup saltine cracker crumbs
¼ cup flour seasoned with salt and pepper

TO FRY

Vegetable oil

GARNISH

Lemon wedges

METHOD

Clean the crabs and remove the gills and sandbags, as well as the small pointed piece on the back of the shell. Soak the crabs in a solution of 2 tablespoons salt dissolved in 1 cup of water for 15 minutes or more. Combine the saltine cracker crumbs with the seasoned flour. Drain the crabs. Dip first in the beaten egg, then roll in the cracker crumbs to coat. Fry in a small amount of oil, heated to 365°F, until golden brown, turning once. This will take 10-15 minutes. Drain on paper towels. Garnish with lemon wedges and serve on toasted triangles of bread. The entire crab is edible.

LIBBY THOMPSON,
GOURMET GALLEY,
PALM BEACH, FL

CLAMS WITH WHITE WINE SAUCE

Preparation Time: 15 minutes
Cooking Time: 20 minutes
Serves: 4

INGREDIENTS

4 dozen clams, well scrubbed
1 cup cold water
2 tsps shallots, chopped
1 tsp garlic, chopped
4oz butter
1 cup dry white wine
Freshly ground pepper to taste
Lemon juice to taste
2 tsps fresh parsley, chopped

METHOD

Steam the clams in the water until they open, approximately 5-10 minutes. Discard any that remain closed. Place the clams in a serving bowl and strain and reserve the cooking liquid. Sauté the shallots and garlic in 2oz of the butter for about 5 minutes — do not allow them to brown. Stir in the reserved liquid and the white wine. Bring to the boil and simmer for 5 minutes. Beat in the remaining butter gradually. Do not allow

Right: Clams with White Wine Sauce.

the sauce to boil. Season with freshly ground pepper and lemon juice. Stir in the chopped parsley and pour the sauce over the clams to serve. Serve these delicious clams in bowls, so that guests can savor the rich sauce.

CHEF HEINZ EBERHARD,
GOURMET GALLEY,
PALM BEACH, FL

FLORIDA SEAFOOD STEW

This stew makes excellent use of the great variety of Florida's famous seafood. The types of fish and shellfish used can be varied, so make use of the types which are freshest in your area.

Preparation Time: 45 minutes
Cooking Time: 1 hour 15 minutes (including stock)
Serves: 8-10

INGREDIENTS

FISH STOCK
1 quart cold water
2lbs fish bones and fish heads
2 onions, coarsely chopped
2 sprigs parsley, chopped
3-4 celery tops, coarsely chopped
Juice of ½ lemon
Salt and freshly ground pepper to taste

STEW
1 tbsp butter
⅓ cup olive oil
1 tbsp fresh garlic, minced
4 tbsps onion, chopped
2 tomatoes, peeled, seeded and chopped
1 tbsp tomato paste
1 tbsp fresh parsley, chopped
Pinch thyme, saffron and oregano
Salt and freshly ground pepper to taste
2-3lbs fresh fish, boned and cut into chunks
2-3lbs shellfish, such as lobster, shrimp, crab, clams or scallops, cleaned, but left in their shells
3oz cognac or brandy
1½ cups dry white wine

METHOD

First prepare the fish stock by combining the fish bones and heads with the water in a large pot. Bring to the boil and add the remaining ingredients. Simmer for 1 hour, skimming as

necessary. Strain and set aside. If the stock is made well in advance, keep refrigerated until needed. To prepare the stew, heat the olive oil and butter in a large frying pan. Add the onions, garlic, parsley, tomatoes, tomato paste and seasonings. Sauté for 3-4 minutes, then add the fish and shellfish. Stir and cook for another 1-2 minutes. Pour the cognac over the seafood. Ignite and allow to flame briefly. Transfer the stew to a stew pot, add the white wine and the fish stock. Simmer for another ten minutes before serving.

CHEF HEINZ EBERHARD,
GOURMET GALLEY,
PALM BEACH, FL

MUSTARD SAUCE

This is a delicious contrasting sauce to serve with cooked seafood.

Preparation Time: 5 minutes
Yield: 1 cup

INGREDIENTS

1 tsp English mustard powder
1 tsp Dijon mustard
1 cup mayonnaise
Juice of ¼ lemon

METHOD

Whip together all the ingredients.

LIBBY THOMPSON AND SYLVIA RICE,
GOURMET GALLEY,
PALM BEACH, FL

FLORIDA LOBSTER MEDALLIONS

The lobster medallions make a spectacular centerpiece to the Gourmet Galley Raw Bar.

Preparation Time: 45 minutes
Cooking Time: 10 minutes
Serves: 4 as an appetizer

Facing page: Florida Seafood Stew.

INGREDIENTS

1 whole lobster
½lb cream cheese, softened

GARNISH

Black olives, sliced
Fresh parsley

METHOD

Place the whole lobster in salted water to cover and bring to the boil. Boil for approximately 5 minutes, or until the lobster turns bright red. Cool, then slit the underside of the tail. Remove the meat, being careful not to cut through the hard top shell. Cut the meat into large, bite-size morsels. Attach the morsels in rows to the top of the lobster shell using the softened cream cheese. Garnish with slices of black olives and parsley.

CHEF HEINZ EBERHARD,
GOURMET GALLEY,
PALM BEACH, FL

SMOKED FISH SPREAD

Preparation Time: 15 minutes
Serves: 3-4

INGREDIENTS

1lb smoked marlin, or other smoked fish, flaked
1 tbsp fresh chives, chopped
1 tbsp minced celery
1 tbsp lemon juice
¼-½ cup mayonnaise
¼ tsp pepper
⅛ tsp salt

METHOD

Combine all the ingredients and mix well. Serve this irresistible spread on crackers. It goes down well with pre-dinner drinks.

CHEF HEINZ EBERHARD,
GOURMET GALLEY,
PALM BEACH, FL

Left: a spectacular seafood arrangement featuring Florida Lobster Madallions.

ROAST LEG OF LAMB

Preparation Time: 15 minutes
Cooking Time: 1½-2 hours
Serves: 6-8

INGREDIENTS

1 5-6lb leg of lamb
6 cloves garlic, crushed
3-4 tbsps dried rosemary
Salt and pepper to taste
Several sprigs fresh rosemary

METHOD

Preheat the oven to 450°F. Rub the lamb with salt, pepper, crushed garlic and dried rosemary. Place the meat in a roasting pan and lay sprigs of fresh rosemary on top. Brown the lamb in the hot oven for approximately 15 minutes, or until the meat is sealed, then lower the temperature to 350°F and roast for about 10 minutes per pound (roughly 1¼-1½ hours total).

The rosemary and garlic enhance the delicious flavor of the lamb. The cooking time suggested will produce a medium-rare roast. If you prefer your meat a bit more done, increase the cooking time slightly.

ART SMITH, GOVERNOR'S MANSION,
TALLAHASSEE, FL

Above: Roast Leg of Lamb.
Facing page: Everglades Frog Legs with Scampi Butter à la Heinz.

FLORIDA DEVILED BLUE CRAB

This deviled crab creation makes a wonderful first course or a tasty light luncheon dish.

Preparation Time: 15 minutes
Cooking Time: 10-15 minutes
Serves: 6-8

INGREDIENTS

2 eggs, beaten
½ cup light cream
2 tbsps melted butter
3 tbsps green pepper, chopped
3 tbsps red pepper, chopped
1 tsp onion, minced

2 cups cooked crab meat, minced or flaked
½ cup bread or cracker crumbs
¼ tsp pepper
⅛ tsp salt

GARNISH

Bread or cracker crumbs
Melted butter

METHOD

Combine all the ingredients and mix well. Use the mixture to fill crab shells or individual butter baking dishes. Garnish with additional crumbs and drizzle with butter. Bake at 350°F for 10-15 minutes, or until lightly browned.

LIBBY THOMPSON, GOURMET GALLEY,
PALM BEACH, FL

EVERGLADES FROG LEGS WITH SCAMPI BUTTER A LA HEINZ

This is a delicious and original way to serve those famous Everglades frog legs. For a picnic you can prepare the frog legs and scampi butter in advance, then heat the dish in a skillet over a campfire or barbecue before serving.

Preparation Time: 20 minutes
Cooking Time: 20 minutes
Serves: 4-6

INGREDIENTS

3-4lbs medium-size frog legs
2 eggs, beaten
¼ cup milk
¼-½ cup flour
Salt and freshly ground pepper to taste

2oz butter
¼ cup cooking oil

SCAMPI BUTTER

1lb butter, at room temperature
1 cup dry white wine
4 tbsps tarragon vinegar
1 tbsp Worcestershire sauce
1 tbsp minced garlic
3 tbsps fresh shallots, minced
2 tbsps fresh chives, minced
2 tbsps onion, minced
1 tbsp fresh parsley, chopped
Salt and freshly ground pepper to taste

METHOD

Season the flour with salt and pepper to taste. In a separate bowl, beat together the eggs and milk. Dip the frog legs first in the egg mixture, then roll in the seasoned flour to coat. Melt the butter and oil in a frying pan and fry the frog legs until they are golden brown. This will take about 1½-2 minutes on each side. Drain on paper towels. Prepare the scampi butter by whipping the softened butter until creamy. Gradually beat in the wine and vinegar, then mix in the remaining ingredients. Arrange the fried frog legs in a shallow casserole and coat generously with the scampi butter. Heat under the broiler or in a very hot oven until heated through.

CHEF HEINZ EBERHARD,
GOURMET GALLEY,
PALM BEACH, FL

LAKE OKEECHOBEE CATFISH

Preparation Time: 20 minutes
Cooking Time: 15-20 minutes
Serves: 4

INGREDIENTS

4 catfish
1 egg, beaten
¼ cup flour
¾ cup cornmeal
2 tbsps butter
2 tbsps vegetable oil

METHOD

Clean and skin the fish and remove the heads. Combine the flour and cornmeal. Dip the fish first in the beaten egg and then in the flour mixture until well coated. Heat the butter and oil in a frying pan. Fry the fish, turning once, until they are golden brown.

The cornmeal coating makes this fish extra tasty and crisp. If catfish is not available, why not try this method using another fish. Serve with lemon wedges and tartare sauce.

LIBBY THOMPSON,
GOURMET GALLEY,
PALM BEACH, FL

CORN BREAD

The addition of the cream-style corn makes this special corn bread extra moist and delicious.

Preparation Time: 15 minutes
Cooking Time: 25 minutes
Yield: 1 9x13-inch bread

INGREDIENTS

3 cups white cornmeal
1 cup flour
4 tbsps sugar
2 tbsps baking powder
1 tsp salt
½ cup vegetable oil
1½ cups cream-style corn
2 cups buttermilk

METHOD

Sift together the dry ingredients, then add the oil, eggs, milk and corn. Mix well. Bake in a greased 9x13 inch pan for 25-30 minutes or until golden. Be careful not to overcook.

LIZ WILLIAMS, GOVERNOR'S MANSION,
TALLAHASSEE, FL

SEAFOOD KEBABS

These colorful kebabs make an attractive and delicious meal for a barbecue, Florida-style.

Preparation Time: 30 minutes
Cooking Time: 5-10 minutes

INGREDIENTS

½ lb seafood pieces per person, including:
Cubes of Florida snapper
Cubes of Florida tile fish
Shrimp
Shelled sea scallops
An assortment of vegetables, including:
Green peppers, cut into wide strips
Red peppers, cut into wide strips
Yellow peppers, cut into wide strips
Cherry tomatoes

MARINADE
½ cup lemon juice
½ cup lime juice
1 tbsp mixed dried herbs
Salt and pepper to taste

Facing page: Lake Okeechobee Catfish.

TO COOK
Melted butter

M E T H O D

Combine the marinade ingredients and marinate the seafood for approximately 30 minutes. Thread the seafood and vegetables on skewers. Brush the kebabs with butter and grill over charcoal for 3-5 minutes on each side, turning frequently.

CHEF HEINZ EBERHARD,
GOURMET GALLEY,
PALM BEACH, FL

Lemon Cream Sherbet

Preparation Time: 15 minutes
Freezing Time: 3½ hours
Yield: approximately 2 pints

I N G R E D I E N T S

Juice and grated rind of 4 large lemons
1¾ cups sugar
2½ cups milk
1 pint half and half

M E T H O D

Combine the lemon juice, rind and sugar in a bowl and leave to stand for 1 hour or more to allow the flavor to develop. Stir in the milk and half and half and mix well. Pour the mixture into freezer trays and freeze for approximately 2½ hours. Spoon the frozen mixture into a bowl and beat until creamy. Return the sherbet to the freezer trays and freeze until firm, about 1 hour. This refreshing sherbet makes an elegant dessert when served in shells made out of the hollowed peels of lemons and garnished with a sprig of fresh mint. A few ripe strawberries arranged on the serving platter make a pleasing contrast.

LIBBY THOMPSON AND SYLVIA RICE,
GOURMET GALLEY,
PALM BEACH, FL

Lemon Cream Sherbet (left), Smoked Fish Spread (bottom center) and Clams with White Wine Sauce (right).

GEORGIA

Georgia, named for King George II of England, is the oldest and one of the most populous of the southern states. The largest state east of the Mississippi River, Georgia presents a varied landscape ranging from the flat coastal plain along the Atlantic, characterized by swamps, pine forests, and gracious ante-bellum towns, to the low, rolling, hills of the central Piedmont district and the rugged mountains and lakes of the Blue Ridge Mountains.

Until the early eighteenth century, Georgia was occupied by the Cherokee and Chocktaw Indians, although the area had been visited by the explorer Hernando do Soto in 1540, and the Spanish had established a chain of missions along the coast. In 1732, George II, wary of Spanish expansionism and the presence of the French colony in Louisiana, granted a charter to James Oglethorpe, an aristocrat and idealist from Godalming, in England, to establish a colony in Georgia. Oglethorpe envisioned a Utopia where the unemployed and the imprisoned debtors could begin a new life. Oglethorpe landed at Savannah in 1733 and began building the planned city. He dreamed of a colony free of the evils of slavery and drunkenness and planned an economy based on sericulture and wine growing. The settlement prospered, but not as Oglethorpe had imagined. The community attracted other dreamers and outcasts from Europe, including large groups of Spanish and Portuguese Jews, and the beautiful city of Savannah became an important center for export to Europe and a principal supply depot for the Confederacy during the Civil War.

Georgia representatives signed the Declaration of Independence in 1775, and in 1788 Georgia became the fourth of the original thirteen colonies to ratify the U. S. Constitution and be admitted to the Union. Georgia seceded from the

Union in 1861, at the start of the Civil War, a conflict that ravaged the economy of the state. But Georgians have always been at the forefront of the economic revival of the New South, and the abundant resources in the state allowed it to recover, diversify, and prosper.

Georgia, the home of Coca-Cola™, is a state whose modern and fast-paced cities are a contrast to the rural lifestyle which still survives in the surrounding areas. But when it comes to food, all the charm and heritage of the Old South is alive and well; Southern fried chicken, barbecue, and country ham reign supreme. Georgia is famous for her peaches, poultry, fresh vegetables, pecans and, above all, her peanuts—made even more prominent by Georgia's favorite son, Jimmy Carter, the 39th President of the United States.

Peanuts, not true nuts but underground legumes, are high in valuable proteins. George Washington Carver may have saved the agricultural economy of the South from collapse when the cotton crop failed after the boll weevil infestation of 1919 by devising 285 new uses for peanuts, but it is the cooks of Georgia who have devised the most delicious and creative uses for the "goober peas" of the old marching song. Everyone loves fresh-roasted peanuts, but in Georgia they put peanuts to an even better use—in peanut soup.

The expression "Thar's gold in them thar hills" originated in northwestern Georgia, which was the site of America's first gold rush. For cooks, Georgia produces another form of gold, her famous peaches. Peach pie is a Georgia tradition, and every cook has his or her own version. Sometimes the peaches are baked in a custard filling, but many prefer their peach pie fried. Pecans are famous too, and the baking of fruit cakes is a major industry in Claxton, in eastern Georgia.

Old southern favorites such as corn bread, collard greens, and chicken and dumplings are as popular in Georgia as they are in the rest of the South. But Georgia cooks take good home cooking even further when they turn their hands to peaches, pecans, and peanuts. James Oglethorpe envisioned that his Utopian colony would be a land of plenty, and as you will see in this collection of recipes gathered in Milledgeville, the state capital from 1807 to 1867, and in Atlanta, the state capital today, this part of his prophecy certainly has come true.

Facing page: Georgia Peach Pie.

COOKING A PIG

If you are planning a really big celebration, you might be interested to know how to cook a pig, Georgia style. This method was developed by Bennett Brown's father.

METHOD

The first point to consider is the pig itself. The ideal pig is one which has been either Federal or State approved, with a dressed (gutted, without head or feet) weight of 110-130lbs. The pig should be split down the breastbone, or butterflied, but not cut in two. Trim away any excess fat in the pig's inner cavity, then liberally salt the entire cavity. This will help to control bacteria and add flavor.

The best way to cook the pig is in a barbecue pit. An easy and inexpensive pit to build is one made of cinder blocks. The pit should be four feet long, four feet wide and three feet deep, with a hole at one end big enough for a shovel to pass through. Make a cooking rack or grill out of metal, preferably stainless steel. The pit may be covered with a piece of plywood.

About ⅓ of a cord of seasoned hardwood, such as oak, hickory, pecan or mesquite, will be needed for the fire which will produce the coals needed for the cooking. Be sure to build the fire in such a way that the coals will be easy to reach through the hole with a shovel.

Build the fire well in advance and prime the pit by heating the grill for 15 minutes. This is similar to preheating an oven and will also kill any bacteria present on the grill. Place the pig on the grill, rib side down. Arrange the coals under the two hams and two shoulders, which are the thickest parts of the pig. It is important to keep a good heat (250-350°F) under the pig at all times, so add new hot coals approximately every 30 minutes. Be careful not to burn the underside of the meat.

The pig should be ready to turn after 10 or more hours, depending on size. After turning, the pig needs constant attention. The heat of the coals will make the back fat liquify and accumulate in the middle rib area. This must be ladled away and discarded, but be careful, the fat is very flammable. During the last three hours, baste the pig with a good barbecue sauce to keep the meat from drying out. When most of the back fat has been rendered, which will take about 5 hours, the pig should be fully cooked. The pig should be cooked enough so that the meat falls off the bone. The pig will serve about 120 people.

BENNETT A BROWN III,
LOWCOUNTRY BARBEQUE CATERING,
ATLANTA, GA

CORN IN THE SHUCK

Southern cooks have developed special methods to preserve the wonderful fresh flavor of summer vegetables. Here is an example.

METHOD

Cut off the top 2 inches of an ear of corn to remove the silk. Remove the outer leaves of the shuck down to the fresh green leaves. Boil the ears in a covered pot for one hour. Remove from the water and pull back the shuck enough to wrap a napkin around it and use it as a handle. Dip the corn in melted butter, then salt and pepper to taste. Corn cooked in this way will retain all of its delicious natural flavor.

BENNETT A BROWN III,
LOWCOUNTRY BARBEQUE CATERING,
ATLANTA, GA

BRUNSWICK STEW

The long, slow cooking of meat and vegetables is characteristic of Southern cooking and makes for a very flavorful result.

Preparation Time: 1 hour
Cooking Time: 4 hours 15 minutes
Serves: 12

INGREDIENTS

2½lb chicken, cut into pieces
1lb beef, diced
1½lbs pork, diced
1½ quarts tomatoes, chopped
1½lbs potatoes
½lb corn on the cob
¾lb onions
½lb lima beans
½lb okra
½lb carrots
1½ quarts water
1 pint ketchup
Salt and pepper to taste

METHOD

Place the meat in a large kettle, cover with water and boil until the meat is well cooked and falling off the bone, approximately 2 hours. Drain the meat, remove from the bones and grind. Set aside. Clean and dice the potatoes, onions, okra and carrots, but leave the lima beans and the corn on the cob whole. Place the water in an 8-quart pot and add all of the vegetables, including the tomatoes. Boil, uncovered, for 1½ hours. Mix in the ketchup, then slowly add the ground meat, stirring constantly. Cook over a medium heat for 45 minutes. Season to taste with salt and pepper before serving.

BENNETT A BROWN III,
LOWCOUNTRY BARBEQUE CATERING,
ATLANTA, GA

COLESLAW

The unusual salad dressing, delicately flavored with dill, makes this coleslaw something special.

Preparation Time: 30 minutes
Serves: 6-8

INGREDIENTS

1 medium cabbage, shredded
3 carrots, shredded

DRESSING

¾ cup mayonnaise
1oz red wine vinegar
½ tbsp dill
¼ tsp salt
⅛ tsp pepper

METHOD

Combine the shredded carrots and cabbage in a large bowl. To prepare the dressing, blend all the dressing ingredients together in a separate bowl until smooth. Pour this dressing over the shredded vegetables and toss until well coated. Chill well before serving.

ANN DORSEY, FULL SERVICE CATERING,
ATLANTA, GA

Facing page: Corn Bread Muffins and Corn in the Shuck are the ideal accompaniment to Barbecued Pig served with Coleslaw and Baked Vidalia Onions.

BAKED VIDALIA ONIONS

Vidalia onions are large, sweet onions which are flat at both ends. They are grown in the area surrounding Vidalia, Georgia and are delicious eaten raw.

M E T H O D

To prepare, peel off the outer skin of the onion and cut a thin slice off both ends so that the onion will sit flat. Cut a small well into one end. Place a bouillon cube inside and cover with a pat of butter. Wrap the onion with a square of heavy aluminum foil. Place the wrapped onions on a baking sheet and bake at 350°F for 1½-2 hours, or until the onion is soft. Loosen the foil and transfer the onion to a small bowl using a slotted spoon. Pour the juices over the onion to serve.

ANN DORSEY, FULL SERVICE CATERING,
ATLANTA, GA

LOWCOUNTRY BARBECUE SAUCE

A spicy sauce, similar to this one, is one of the Brown family secrets.

Preparation Time: 15 minutes
Cooking Time: 25 minutes
Yield: approximately 1 quart

I N G R E D I E N T S

1 quart apple cider vinegar
1 pint ketchup
½ tbsp Worcestershire sauce
2 tbsps black pepper
¼ tsp cayenne pepper

½ tbsp salt
1 tbsp sugar

METHOD

Boil the vinegar for approximately 10 minutes, then stir in the ketchup and Worcestershire sauce. Reduce the heat to medium and mix in the black and red pepper, salt and sugar. Simmer over a low heat for 15 minutes, stirring often.

BENNETT A BROWN III,
LOWCOUNTRY BARBEQUE CATERING,
ATLANTA, GA

Facing page: Baked Vidalia Onions and (below) Lowcountry Barbecue Sauce.

GEORGIA PEANUT SOUP

This unusual soup makes delicious use of Georgia's famous peanuts.

Preparation Time: 15 minutes
Cooking Time: 25 minutes
Serves: 4-6

INGREDIENTS

2 tbsps butter
1 stalk celery, finely chopped
1 medium onion, finely chopped
1 tbsp flour
4 cups chicken stock
½ cup chunky peanut butter
1½ cups half and half or milk
Salt and pepper to taste

GARNISH

¼ cup chopped peanuts
Paprika

M E T H O D

In a large saucepan, melt the butter over a low heat. Add the celery and onion and sauté until they are softened but not brown. Stir in the flour to make a smooth paste and cook for 2-3 minutes. Gradually add the chicken stock, stirring to make a smooth sauce. Bring the soup to a boil. Blend in the peanut butter and simmer for about 15 minutes, stirring occasionally. Add the half and half to the pan and heat the soup just to the boiling point. Taste and add salt and pepper if necessary. To serve, garnish each bowl of soup with chopped peanuts and a sprinkling of paprika.

SARALYN LATHAM, THE WILLIS HOUSE,
MILLEDGEVILLE, GA

SPECIAL YEAST ROLLS

These tasty light yeast rolls are a great favorite with visitors.

Preparation Time: 20 minutes plus 2 hours rising
time
Cooking Time: 12 minutes
Yield: approximately 36-48

I N G R E D I E N T S

1 cup hot water
6 tbsps shortening
1 tsp salt
⅓ cup sugar
1½ packages (1½ tbsps) dried yeast, dissolved in 3 tbsps
lukewarm water
1 egg, at room temperature, lightly beaten
3½-4½ cups flour, sifted twice

METHOD

Combine the hot water, salt, shortening and sugar in a large bowl and mix thoroughly using a wooden spoon. Allow to cool to lukewarm, then add the egg, yeast and half of the flour. Mix well and add enough flour so that the mixture is no longer sticky, using more flour than specified if necessary. Knead the dough 4 or 5 times with your hands, then place it in a well-greased airtight container and refrigerate for at least an hour. If you wish, the dough may be stored for up to one week.

To bake, flour your hands and pull off small pieces of dough and shape into rolls. You may add flour if the dough is sticky. Place the rolls on greased baking trays and leave to rise for 1½ to 2 hours. Bake at 400°F for 10-12 minutes, or until golden brown.

SARALYN LATHAM, THE WILLIS HOUSE,
MILLEDGEVILLE, GA

Facing page: Georgia Peanut Soup. Below: Biscuits (bottom left) and Corn Bread (right).

CORN BREAD

Preparation Time: 15 minutes
Cooking Time: 20 minutes
Yield: 1 9×9 inch bread

INGREDIENTS

2 cups self-rising cornmeal or
2 cups cornmeal plus 3 tsps baking powder
3 tbsps flour
1 tbsp sugar
¼ cup + 2 tbsps vegetable oil
1¾ cups buttermilk
1 egg
3-4 tbsps bacon drippings

METHOD

Combine all the ingredients except for the bacon drippings and blend well. Bake in a preheated, greased 9×9 inch pan for 20 minutes at 425°F. Spoon the bacon drippings on top, return to the oven and bake until brown. The addition of bacon drippings adds a delicious new twist to an old Southern favorite.

SARALYN LATHAM, THE WILLIS HOUSE,
MILLEDGEVILLE, GA

CORN BREAD MUFFINS

Preparation Time: 20 minutes
Cooking Time: 20 minutes
Yield: 18

INGREDIENTS

1½ cups yellow cornmeal
1 cup flour
½ cup sugar
1 tbsp baking powder
1 tsp salt
1½ cups milk
¾ cup butter, melted and cooled slightly
2 eggs, lightly beaten

METHOD

Combine the cornmeal, flour, sugar, baking powder and salt in a large bowl. In a separate bowl, combine the milk, butter

Above: Corn Bread Muffins. Facing page: Chicken and Dumplings.

and eggs. Stir the milk mixture into the dry ingredients until just moistened. Leave the batter to stand for about ten minutes, then pour the mixture into greased muffin tins. Bake for 18-20 minutes, or until golden.

For a tasty variation, try adding 1 cup of whole kernel corn to the batter.

ANN DORSEY, FULL SERVICE CATERING,
ATLANTA, GA

CHICKEN AND DUMPLINGS

Chicken and Dumplings brings all the warmth and friendliness of a Georgia country kitchen home to you.

Preparation Time: 20 minutes
Cooking Time: 2½-3½ hours
Serves: 6-8

INGREDIENTS

1 large boiling hen
4oz butter
Water to cover
Salt and pepper to taste

DUMPLINGS

4 cups plain flour
1½ cups ice water

GARNISH

Fresh or dried parsley

METHOD

Place the hen and the butter in a large pot and pour over water to cover. Boil for 2-3 hours, or until the hen is very tender,

adding extra water if necessary. Remove the hen and allow to cool, reserving the broth. When the hen is cool enough to handle, remove the bones, cut the meat into serving-size pieces and return to the broth. To prepare the dumplings, make a well in the middle of the flour. Pour in the ice water and blend with a fork or with your fingers until the dough forms a ball. Roll out thinly and cut into 2-3-inch-wide strips. Bring the chicken and broth to the boil and season to taste with salt and pepper. Slowly drop the dough strips into the broth. Simmer for 2-4 minutes, or until the dumplings are tender. Serve immediately, garnished with dried or fresh parsley.

SARALYN LATHAM, THE WILLIS HOUSE, MILLEDGEVILLE, GA

CHICKEN AND SEAFOOD ROLL-UPS

These are delicious served with a mushroom cream sauce for a special occasion.

Preparation Time: 30 minutes
Cooking Time: 20-25 minutes
Serves: 8

INGREDIENTS

8 chicken breasts, boned
2 cups stuffing, such as seasoned bread or corn bread crumbs, moistened with stock
1 cup shrimp, cooked and sliced in half
8oz crab meat
1 cup flour, seasoned with salt and pepper
4 eggs, beaten
1 cup milk
12oz butter

METHOD

Combine the stuffing, shrimp and crab meat. Spoon this mixture over the chicken breasts. Roll up the chicken, tucking the ends inside. Dip the rolls first in the beaten eggs, then in flour, then in the milk, then in flour again. Melt the butter

Sweet Potato Soufflé (left) and Chicken and Seafood Roll-Ups (right).

in a skillet until bubbling. Gently brown the roll-ups, then drain and place them in an oiled baking pan. Bake at 350°F for 20-25 minutes.

SARALYN LATHAM, THE WILLIS HOUSE,
MILLEDGEVILLE, GA

SWEET POTATO SOUFFLÉ

Southerners like their sweet potatoes sweet. Try this as a special accompaniment to a Thanksgiving turkey.

Preparation Time: 40 minutes
Cooking Time: 15-20 minutes
Serves: 4-6

INGREDIENTS

1½lbs sweet potatoes, washed, but not peeled
1 egg
1oz margarine
1¼ cups sugar
1 tbsp evaporated milk
2 tsps vanilla

TOPPING

¾ cup light brown sugar
1½oz margarine, melted
¼ cup pecans

METHOD

Boil the sweet potatoes until they are soft. Peel them while they are still hot, and place them in the large bowl of an electric mixer. Mix at low speed and add the remaining ingredients. Place this mixture in a large baking dish. To prepare the topping, combine all of the topping ingredients. Spread over the potatoes and bake at 375°F for approximately 15-20 minutes, or until set.

SARALYN LATHAM, THE WILLIS HOUSE,
MILLEDGEVILLE, GA

COLLARDS

Collards are often cooked all day over a low heat, ready to serve up as an accompaniment to meat.

Preparation Time: 20 minutes
Cooking Time: approximately 3½ hours
Serves: 6-8

INGREDIENTS

2-3 bunches fresh collards
4 pieces ham hock
Salt to taste

METHOD

Boil the ham hock in water to cover for approximately 1-1½ hours. Clean the collards very thoroughly and remove the tough stems. Add the collards to the ham hocks and water and continue cooking for a further 2 hours or until tender. Season well with salt.

SARALYN LATHAM, THE WILLIS HOUSE,
MILLEDGEVILLE, GA

FRIED GREEN TOMATOES

Here is a delicious way to use the tomatoes in your garden which don't turn red.

METHOD

Use firm green tomatoes. Wash and slice the tomatoes crosswise into ½-inch-thick slices. Dredge the slices in a mixture of two parts cornmeal and 1 part flour. Heat ½ cup oil and ¼ cup butter in a heavy skillet to a medium high heat. Place the coated slices in the skillet and sprinkle with a few pinches of sugar. Turn the slices when the undersides are golden brown and sprinkle with fresh ground black pepper. Continue cooking for a few more minutes, then remove the tomatoes to a paper towel to drain. Serve immediately.

ANN DORSEY, FULL SERVICE CATERING,
ATLANTA, GA

BISCUITS

These biscuits taste best if served fresh from the oven. This recipe makes enough biscuits to serve the Confederate Army! If you are dealing with a smaller crowd, try using quarter quantities.

Germans, Scots-Irish, Sephardic Jews, and Welshmen. When slaves were introduced to the area in 1671, the cultivation of rice began in the low, swampy country around Charleston. The economy of the state remained agriculturally based until the Second World War.

Charleston, located on the peninsula formed by the Cooper River, was the only town in the state until 1730, and the only real city in the South during the eighteenth century. During its golden age, from 1740 to 1778, Charleston was the cultural capital of Colonial America. Wealthy planters of rice and indigo lived in modest plantation houses in the surrounding countryside during the winter, but came to Charleston in the summer, where they lived a life of elegance in their magnificent summer homes.

Today, Charleston remains one of the most charming and visually exciting cities in the South, with its rows of white houses with long, double-story piazzas running from the street front through to the gardens that line the streets surrounding the harbor area. Traditional eating habits still survive in parts of the city where summer breakfasts consist of grits, boiled shrimp, and tomatoes, and where weekday dinners, served at 2 o'clock—the old English hour—are followed by a siesta.

The cooking of South Carolina has been greatly influenced by the many immigrants who settled in Charleston. In this collection of recipes from the Junior League of Charleston, the influence of the French Huguenots, reflected in dishes such as egg soufflé, Huguenot torte, and French biscuits, is particularly strong. Locally grown rice is served with many meals. One traditional method of cooking is to brown the rice in butter before pouring boiling water or stock over it and baking it in a covered casserole.

South Carolina is famous for its seafood specialties. Shrimp is a breakfast favorite, especially in the low country, and many of the breakfast recipes have been handed down for generations. The simplest way to prepare breakfast shrimp is to sauté them in melted butter and serve them hot, always with hominy. Seafood is popular at other meals, too. Dishes made with low country oysters are plentiful, and crab meat served in many different forms abounds.

Facing page: Huguenot Torte.

FRANCIS MARION RECEPTION PUNCH

This non-alcoholic punch is named after the teetotaller Francis Marion, the revolutionary hero also known as the "Swamp Fox". However, this punch can also be used as the basis for an alcoholic punch by substituting 4 quarts of your favorite alcoholic beverage for the pineapple juice.

Preparation Time: 15 minutes
Serves: 100

INGREDIENTS

1 quart frozen orange juice
3 quarts ice water
Juice of 18 lemons or 6oz frozen lemon juice
4 quarts pineapple juice
4 quarts carbonated water or ginger ale

METHOD

Prepare the "stock" by combining the orange juice, ice water, lemon juice and pineapple juice. Mix thoroughly and chill. To serve, pour half of the stock into a large punch bowl and add two quarts of the carbonated water or ginger ale. Use the rest of the stock and carbonated water as needed to keep the punch "alive". The punch may be sweetened with sugar dissolved in water, if desired.

MRS. KATHERINE HERMAN,
CHARLESTON, SC
(FROM "CHARLESTON RECEIPTS,"
COMPILED AND EDITED BY THE JUNIOR
LEAGUE OF CHARLESTON, INC.)

MEETING STREET CRAB MEAT

This tasty seafood dish may also be made with shrimp. Use 1½lbs raw, peeled shrimp in place of the crab meat.

Preparation Time: 20 minutes
Cooking Time: 15 minutes
Serves: 4

Francis Marion Reception Punch.

Facing page: She-Crab Soup and (above) Meeting Street Crab Meat.

INGREDIENTS

4 tbsps butter
4 tbsps flour
1 cup cream
4 tbsps sherry
Salt and pepper to taste
1lb white crab meat
¾ cup grated sharp cheese

METHOD

In a saucepan, melt the butter. Gradually stir in the flour to make a smooth paste. Cook for a few minutes over a low heat then gradually stir in the cream. Add the sherry, salt and pepper. Cook over a medium heat, stirring often, until the sauce is thickened. Remove from the heat and stir in the crab meat. Pour the mixture into a buttered casserole, or into 4 individual baking dishes. Sprinkle with the grated cheese and bake at 400°F for approximately 10 minutes, or until the cheese melts. Be careful not to overcook.

MRS. THOMAS A. HUGUENIN,
CHARLESTON, SC
(FROM "CHARLESTON RECEIPTS,"
COMPILED AND EDITED BY THE JUNIOR
LEAGUE OF CHARLESTON, INC.)

SHE-CRAB SOUP

The She-Crab is preferred for this soup because the eggs add a special flavor. If you are unable to obtain female crabs, crumble the yolk of hard-boiled eggs into the bottom of the soup plates before serving.

Preparation Time: 30 minutes
Cooking Time: 20 minutes
Serves: 4-6

INGREDIENTS

1 tbsp butter
1 tsp flour
1 quart milk
2 cups white crab meat and crab eggs
½ tsp Worcestershire sauce
⅛ tsp mace
Few drops onion juice
½ tsp salt
⅛ tsp pepper

TO SERVE

4 tbsps dry sherry, warmed
¼ pint cream, whipped
Paprika or finely chopped parsley

METHOD

In the top of a double boiler, melt the butter and blend in the flour until smooth. Add the milk gradually, stirring constantly. Add the crab meat and eggs and all of the seasonings. Cook the soup slowly for 20 minutes over hot water. To serve, place one tablespoon of warmed sherry in individual soup bowls. Add the soup and top with whipped cream. Sprinkle with paprika or finely chopped parsley.

MRS. HENRY F. CHURCH, CHARLESTON, SC
(FROM "CHARLESTON RECEIPTS,"
COMPILED AND EDITED BY THE JUNIOR
LEAGUE OF CHARLESTON, INC.)

BROWNED RICE

This delicious rice dish goes well with meat or chicken.

Preparation Time: 10 minutes
Cooking Time: 30-40 minutes
Serves: 4

INGREDIENTS

1½ cups rice
2 tbsps butter
3½ cups water

1½ tsps salt
⅛ tsp pepper

TO SERVE

Extra buter or ham drippings
Dash paprika

METHOD

Place the dry rice in a frying pan with the butter and stir over a moderate heat until the rice is golden brown. Add the water and seasonings and bring to the boil. Place the rice in a covered casserole and bake at 350°F for 30-40 minutes or until dry and flaky. To serve, stir in extra butter or ham drippings and a dash of parika. Serve hot.

MRS. PRIOLEAU BALL, CHARLESTON, SC
(FROM "CHARLESTON RECEIPTS,"
COMPILED AND EDITED BY THE JUNIOR
LEAGUE OF CHARLESTON, INC.)

MRS. SAMUEL G. STONEY'S BLACK RIVER PÂTÉ

This is an old French Huguenot dish which has been in the Stoney family for generations.

Preparation Time: 45 minutes
Cooking Time: approximately 1 hour

INGREDIENTS

3 parts leftover venison
1 part butter
Coarse black pepper and salt to taste

METHOD

Put the venison through the finest blade of a meat grinder twice. Work the pepper into the butter and add salt to taste. Combine the venison and seasoned butter in a Pyrex dish and pound with a wooden mallet until the pâté forms a solid mass.

Facing page: Mrs. Samuel G. Stoney's Black River Pâté.

SOUTH CAROLINA

Smooth the top and bake at 325°F for approximately 1 hour, or until golden brown. Chill before serving.

To serve, cut into thin slices and serve with hominy or salad. The pâté will keep indefinitely in the refrigerator.

MRS. WILLIAM S. POPHAM (NEE STONEY)
CHARLESTON, SC
(FROM "CHARLESTON RECEIPTS,"
COMPILED AND EDITED BY THE JUNIOR
LEAGUE OF CHARLESTON, INC.)

POMPANO À LA GHERARDI

This delicious fish dish is an original creation which was named for Admiral Gherardi.

Preparation Time: 45 minutes
Cooking Time: 30 minutes
Serves: 6

INGREDIENTS

6 small pompano
Salt and pepper

STUFFING

1lb cooked shrimp
½lb white crab meat
½ loaf bread
½ bunch green onions
¼ cup sherry
½ cup butter
3 tbsps parsley
1 egg

GARNISH

½lb cooked shrimp
6 strips bacon
½ cup chopped olives

METHOD

Remove the heads of the fish and split down the flat side, removing the backbone and ribs to form a pocket. Sprinkle salt and pepper inside and set aside while you prepare the stuffing.

Pompano à la Gherardi.

To prepare the stuffing, mince together the shrimp, crab meat, bread, green onions, parsley and butter. Stir in the sherry and egg and season to taste with salt and pepper. Cook over a low heat, stirring frequently until heated through, about 10-15 minutes. Use this stuffing to stuff the fish. Top the pocket opening with the garnish of whole cooked shrimp, chopped olives and strips of bacon. Arrange in a covered casserole and bake at 350°F for 15 minutes, or until the fish is fully cooked.

WALTER L. SHAFFER,
HENRY'S RESTAURANT, CHARLESTON, SC
(FROM "CHARLESTON RECEIPTS,"
COMPILED AND EDITED BY THE JUNIOR
LEAGUE OF CHARLESTON, INC.)

LOW COUNTRY OYSTERS WITH MUSHROOMS

Serve these creamy oysters from a chafing dish with triangles of hot buttered toast.

Preparation Time: 30 minutes
Cooking Time: 15 minutes
Serves: 8

INGREDIENTS

1lb fresh mushrooms, sliced
8oz canned pimentos, sliced
8 tbsps butter
8 tbsps flour

Below: Halidon Hill Potted Birds.

Above: Low Country Oysters with Mushrooms.

4 cups cream
1½ quarts oysters, cleaned
Salt and pepper to taste

METHOD

Sauté the mushrooms and pimentos in the butter. After the mushrooms have softened, sift the flour over the pan and stir in. When the sauce begins to thicken, add the cream, salt and pepper. In a separate pan, let the oysters simmer in their own liquor until the edges curl. Add the oysters to the mushroom sauce, stirring in additional cream if the dish seems too dry.

MRS. THOMAS A. HUGUENIN,
CHARLESTON, SC
(FROM "CHARLESTON RECEIPTS,"
COMPILED AND EDITED BY THE JUNIOR
LEAGUE OF CHARLESTON, INC.)

HALIDON HILL POTTED BIRDS

Preparation Time: 30 minutes
Cooking Time: 2-3 hours
Serves: 6

INGREDIENTS

6 Cornish game hens
½ cup flour
Salt and pepper to taste
2½ tbsps lard
Water for cooking
STUFFING
6 slices toasted stale bread, broken into small pieces
¼ small onion, minced
4 slices breakfast bacon
¾ cup hot water
Salt and pepper to taste

METHOD

Begin by preparing the stuffing. Fry the bacon until crisp and break up into small pieces. Add the onion and cook until golden, then stir in the bread, salt, pepper and hot water. Mix well.

Wipe the birds inside and out with a damp cloth, then fill lightly with the stuffing. Sprinkle the birds with the salt, pepper and flour. Melt the lard in a cast iron pot or skillet. Brown the birds, then add a little water and cover tightly. Cook very slowly until tender, 45 minutes–1 hour or more. Add more water if necessary.

The tasty stuffing could also be used to stuff a roast chicken or other larger bird.

MRS. THOMAS A. HUGUENIN,
CHARLESTON, SC
(FROM "CHARLESTON RECEIPTS,"
COMPILED AND EDITED BY THE JUNIOR
LEAGUE OF CHARLESTON, INC.)

MRS. RALPH IZARD'S "AWENDAW"

This old-fashioned dish makes a good accompaniment to meat dishes.

Preparation Time: 20 minutes
Cooking Time: 30-45 minutes
Serves: 6-8

INGREDIENTS

1½ cups cooked hominy
1 tbsp butter
3 eggs, very well beaten
1½ cups milk
¾ cups cornmeal
½ tsp salt

METHOD

While the hominy is still hot, add the butter and the well beaten eggs. Gradually stir in the milk and, when well mixed, add

Facing page: Lady Baltimore Cake.

the cornmeal and the salt. The batter should resemble a thick custard. Pour the batter into a greased deep pan and bake at 375°F for 30-45 minutes, or until set.

MRS. EMMA GAILLARD WITSELL,
CHARLESTON, SC
(FROM "CHARLESTON RECEIPTS,"
COMPILED AND EDITED BY THE JUNIOR
LEAGUE OF CHARLESTON, INC.)

LADY BALTIMORE CAKE

This glamorous cake was made famous in Charleston's Lady Baltimore Tea Room.

Preparation Time: 30 minutes
Cooking Time: 30 minutes
Yield: 1 large cake

INGREDIENTS

1 cup butter
3 cups sugar
4 eggs
1 cup milk
3½ cups cake flour
4 tsps baking powder
2 tsps vanilla
2 tsps almond extract
½ cup water

FROSTING

2 cups sugar
⅔ cup water
2 tsps corn syrup
2 egg whites, beaten stiffly
2 cups seedless raisins, finely chopped and soaked
overnight in sherry or brandy, if desired
2 cups pecans or walnuts, finely chopped
12 figs, finely chopped and soaked overnight in sherry or
brandy, if desired
Almond and vanilla extract, to taste

METHOD

Using an electric mixer, cream the butter. Add 2 cups of the sugar gradually and beat to the consistency of whipped cream. Add the eggs one at a time and beat thoroughly. Sift together the baking powder and flour three times. Add alternately with the milk, using a wooden spoon to blend. Pour the batter into two greased 11-inch cake pans and bake at 350°F for 30 minutes, or until done. While the cakes are baking, make a thick syrup of the remaining cup of sugar and the water. Flavor with the almond and vanilla extract. When the cake is baked, cool in the pans for 10 minutes, then turn the layers out onto a rack for complete cooling. As soon as you remove the layers from the pans, spread the prepared syrup on top.

To prepare the frosting, combine the sugar, water and syrup in a saucepan. Cook until the mixture forms a firm ball when a spoonful is dropped into cold water. Pour this syrup gradually into the stiffly beaten egg whites, beating constantly. Add the raisins, nuts and figs. Finally stir in the almond and vanilla extracts to taste. When the cake is cool, spread this frosting between the layers and on the top and sides of the cake.

MRS. HOWARD READ, CHARLESTON, SC
(FROM "CHARLESTON RECEIPTS,"
COMPILED AND EDITED BY THE JUNIOR
LEAGUE OF CHARLESTON, INC.)

HUGUENOT TORTE

Apples and nuts are a delicious addition to this old-fashioned dessert.

Preparation Time: 20 minutes
Cooking Time: 45 minutes
Serves: 8

INGREDIENTS

2 eggs
1½ cups sugar
4 tbsps flour
2½ cups baking powder
¼ tsp salt
1 cup tart cooking apples, chopped
1 cup chopped pecans or walnuts
1 tsp vanilla

TO SERVE

Whipped cream
Chopped nuts

METHOD

Beat the eggs with an electric or rotary mixer until they are very frothy and lemon-colored. Add the remaining ingredients in the order given. Pour the batter into a well-buttered 8 x

12-inch baking pan. Bake at 325°F for about 45 minutes, or until brown and crusty.

To serve, scoop up portions with a pancake turner, keeping the crusty top uppermost. Cover each serving with whipped cream and a sprinkling of chopped nuts.

MRS. CORNELIUS HUGUENIN,
CHARLESTON, SC
(FROM "CHARLESTON RECEIPTS,"
COMPILED AND EDITED
BY THE JUNIOR LEAGUE OF
CHARLESTON, INC.)

COLONEL AIKEN SIMONS' MINT JULEP

There are many ways to make a mint julep. Here is the formula as devised by Colonel Aiken Simons, and well loved by his descendants.

Preparation Time: approximately 15 minutes

METHOD

Take a pitcher or jug of suitable size and add a teaspoon of sugar for each julep. Add just enough water to dissolve the sugar, about an equal volume of water to sugar is sufficient, if you stir well. Pour in a whiskey glass of bourbon for each julep and stir well. Select 4 or 5 fine sprigs of mint and add them to the mixture. Whether this mint should be crushed or not is a subject of great controversy. It depends on the strength of the mint and the taste of the drinkers. Allow to stand for a while.

To serve, fill each glass with broken ice, taking care not to get the outside of the glass wet. Divide the contents of the pitcher among the glasses and stir each vigorously. Fill up the glasses with more ice and stir again briskly. A thick, white coating of frost should have formed on the glass by now. Handle the glass very carefully to avoid marring the frost, because this is the pride and joy of the julep. Choose very fine sprigs of mint for the garnish; place one in each glass and serve.

ALBERT SIMONS, CHARLESTON, SC

Facing page: Colonel Aiken Simons' Mint Julep.

NORTH CAROLINA

North Carolina, the Tar Heel State, nestled between its two proud neighbors, Virginia to the north and South Carolina to the south, describes itself as "a vale of humility between two mountains of conceit." It remains a small-town state, and the humility for which natives like to be known is reflected in the humble names they have chosen for some of their settlements, such as Bottom, Toast, Whynot, and Lizard Lick. Yet North Carolinians have much to be proud of.

When Giovanni de Verrazzano, the first European to explore the territory, saw the area, he reported that it was "as pleasant and delectable to behold, as is possible to imagine." This remains as true today as it was then. Many Southerners come to vacation here, and become so capitivated by its rural beauty that they end up staying for good.

There are three distinctive geographical regions in the state: the eastern coastal plain, the central Piedmont, and the western mountains, each with its own climate, fauna, flora, and way of life. The majestically flat coastal plain, with its irregular coastline, is protected by a 175-mile string of barrier islands, the Outer Banks. These lovely, hurricane-swept shoals are surrounded by treacherous waters, and many of the inhabitants trace their ancestry to seventeenth- and eighteenth-century shipwreck victims who were unable to go home. The central Piedmont, with its rolling, wooded hills, is in the heart of the tobacco-growing country. The forests of beautiful pines produce the tar, turpentine, and pitch that give the North Carolina Tar Heels their nickname and have provided an income since the early days of settlement. The Blue Ridge and Smoky Mountains in the western part of the state, called the "Great Blue Hills of God" by the native Cherokee Indians, are wonderfully scenic, and famous for their great variety of native fauna and flora.

These diverse areas provide many of the ingredients that have inspired great cooks. The coastal area along the Outer Banks is a fisherman's paradise and the source of abundant fresh seafood, including delicious crab and shrimp. The Scuppernong grape, which makes delicious jams and preserves, is native to the eastern part of the state. The fertile soils of the coastal plain nurture many vegetable crops, ranging from beans to sweet potatoes and peanuts. They all provide food for the kitchen as well as for the poultry and hogs that are raised here. Fresh river fish such as trout, as well as tasty game birds, come from the hills and forests of the central Piedmont and the mountainous region to the west.

The culinary influence of many of the diverse immigrant groups, including the Moravians, a German religious sect who settled near Salem, is marked. Some of their favorite sweets, including citron pie and light, white cream cakes, are now local specialities.

North Carolina cooks also follow the lovingly preserved traditions common to all southern cooks, reflecting a time when local ingredients were cooked to perfection and seasoned with great care. Much use is made of the local seafood and the game birds and fish from the forests and streams of the Piedmont, always carefully seasoned to bring out the best flavors. And, like all other Southerners, North Carolinians eat their share of the traditional cornmeal mush, black-eyed peas, and, of course, biscuits.

Cream, butter, and eggs are in abundant supply and are freely used to enrich all types of dishes. Desserts, especially, benefit from this treatment. A dessert table in North Carolina is a sight to behold! Simple, fruit-based desserts are lavishly embellished with rich, sweet sauces and gorgeous, feather-light cakes with mountains of whipped cream.

The recipes in this collection are representative of the types of dishes served throughout the state. They were gathered in Chapel Hill, a city situated on a hilltop at the eastern edge of the Piedmont plateau. The gracious and serene atmosphere of the area has so delighted residents that they forget their traditional humility and sometimes refer to it as "the Southern part of Heaven." Whether it be heaven or earth, the menus served in North Carolina do seem to have been concocted by angels.

Facing page: Chocolate Mint Torte with Bourbon Crème Anglaise.

PAN-ROASTED QUAIL WITH BLACK-EYED PEAS, VINAIGRETTE AND FRIED CORNMEAL MUSH

If quail are not available, Cornish game hens (one per person) could be prepared in a similar way.

Preparation Time: 30 minutes
Cooking Time: 15-20 minutes
Serves: 4

INGREDIENTS

8 dressed quail, 4½-6oz each

MARINADE

¼ cup molasses
¼ cup bourbon whiskey
½ cup cold-pressed peanut oil
1 tsp salt
2 tbsp fresh tarragon, chopped
2 shallots, finely minced
2 cloves garlic, pressed
6 grinds of fresh black pepper

PAN GRAVY

1 shallot, finely minced
1 clove garlic, finely minced
¾ cup rich chicken stock
1 tsp fresh tarragon, chopped
Salt to taste
Black pepper to taste

GARNISH

Thyme flowers

METHOD

Rinse the quail and pat dry. Combine the marinade ingredients and marinade the quail for at least 6 hours. Remove the quail from the marinade and pat dry before cooking. Heat a small

Strawberry Raspberry Shortcakes (top left), Crab Cakes with Red Pepper and Tomato Sauce (top right), Walter's Fried Okra (bottom left), Pan-Roasted Quail with Black-Eyed Peas, Vinaigrette and Fried Cornmeal Mush (bottom center) and Tomatoes and Cucumbers with Scallions and Dill (bottom right).

amount of peanut oil in a large skillet until it is nearly smoking. Add the quail and brown on both sides over a medium-high heat. Reduce the heat to medium, turn the quail breast side up, and cook, covered, for 5-7 minutes, or until the birds are medium-rare. Keep warm in a slow oven while you prepare the pan gravy.

To make the gravy, pour off all of the fat from the pan in which the quail were cooked. Add the minced garlic and shallot and sauté over a high heat until they are lightly browned. Carefully add the bourbon and ignite. When the flames die down, scrape the bottom of the pan. Add the chicken stock, bring the gravy to the boil and cook until reduced by half. Add the chopped tarragon, then adjust the seasoning with salt and pepper.

To serve the quail, make nests of Black-eyed Peas Vinaigrette on beds of curly endive, escarole or other leafy green vegetable on 4 plates. Place triangles of Fried Cornmeal Mush around the edges of the nests and arrange 2 quail on top of each. Pour pan gravy over the quail and garnish with thyme flowers.

BEN BARKER, FEARRINGTON HOUSE,
CHAPEL HILL, NC

TOMATOES AND CUCUMBERS WITH SCALLIONS AND DILL

This delicious salad makes the best of summer vegetables.

Preparation Time: 45 minutes
Serves: 4-8

INGREDIENTS

*4 large vine-ripened tomatoes,
cut into ½-inch thick slices
1 large cucumber, decoratively scored and
cut into ¼-inch slices
3 scallions, thinly sliced
Coarse salt
Fresh black pepper, coarsely ground*

VINAIGRETTE

*¼ cup cold-pressed peanut oil
3 tbsps cider vinegar
¼ cup chopped dill*

METHOD

First prepare the vinaigrette by combining the vinegar, peanut oil and dill. Place the cucumber slices in the vinaigrette and leave to marinate in the refrigerator for ½ hour. Drain the cucumber, reserving the vinaigrette, and arrange on a platter, overlapping the slices. Arrange the tomato slices on top of the cucumber and sprinkle the chopped scallions over all. Drizzle vinaigrette over the vegetables and sprinkle on coarse salt and fresh coarsely ground black pepper.

BEN BARKER, FEARRINGTON HOUSE,
CHAPEL HILL, NC

WALTER'S FRIED OKRA

This makes a delicious first course, or try serving with meat.

Preparation Time: 15 minutes
Cooking Time: 15-20 minutes
Serves: 6-8

INGREDIENTS

*1lb fresh okra, washed and trimmed
2 cups buttermilk
1½ cups stone-ground yellow cornmeal
½ tsp cayenne pepper
¼ tsp black pepper
⅛ tsp white pepper
½ tsp salt
⅛ tsp paprika
⅛ tsp ground cumin*

TO FRY

4 cups peanut oil

TO SERVE

Lemon wedges

METHOD

Soak the okra in the buttermilk. Meanwhile, combine the cornmeal and the spices. Remove the okra from the buttermilk and roll it in the spiced cornmeal until well coated. Heat the peanut oil in a heavy-bottomed pan to 350°F. Fry the coated okra in batches to a deep golden brown. Drain each batch on absorbent paper and keep warm in a low oven. Serve the fried okra hot with lemon wedges.

WALTER ROYAL, FEARRINGTON HOUSE,
CHAPEL HILL, NC

FRIED CORNMEAL MUSH

Serve this with pan-roasted quail, or to accompany other chicken dishes.

Preparation Time: 15 minutes
Cooking Time: 10-15 minutes
Serves: 4-6

INGREDIENTS

1 quart chicken stock or water
1 cup yellow stone-ground cornmeal
2 tbsps grated Parmesan cheese
2 tbsps chives, minced
1 tsp salt

TO FRY

2 tbsps flour
¼ cup clarified butter

METHOD

Bring 3 cups of the liquid to the boil. Mix the cornmeal with the remaining cup of liquid and pour this mixture into the boiling liquid, stirring well. Continue to cook until a spoon will stand up in the mush. Stir in the Parmesan cheese, chives and salt. Spread the cornmeal mush over a buttered cookie sheet to a ½-inch thickness. Cool completely, then cut into triangles. Dust the triangles with flour and sauté them in clarified butter until they are golden brown on both sides.

ADAPTED FROM MADELEINE KAMMAN'S
"IN MADELEINE'S KITCHEN" BY
FEARRINGTON HOUSE, CHAPEL HILL, NC

NORTH CAROLINA SHRIMP BOIL

Preparation Time: 5 minutes
Cooking Time: approximately 25 minutes
Serves: 4

INGREDIENTS

2lbs large shrimp with the heads left on
1½ tbsps crushed red pepper flakes
1 tsp whole black peppercorns
1 tsp dried oregano
1 tsp dried basil
1 tsp dried thyme
2 large bay leaves
2 tbsps coarse salt
2 lemons, cut in half
12oz beer
4 quarts cold water

TO SERVE

Lemon wedges
Red pepper mayonnaise

METHOD

Combine the herbs, lemon, beer and water in a 1 gallon pot. Bring to a boil and simmer for 15 minutes. Return the mixture to the boil, add the shrimp, cover and cook for 1 minute. Drain immediately. Serve the shrimp hot on newspapers and allow guests to peel their own, or chill the shrimp, then peel and arrange on individual plates.

Serve with lots of lemon wedges, and pass Red Pepper Mayonnaise separately.

BEN BARKER, FEARRINGTON HOUSE,
CHAPEL HILL, NC

RED PEPPER MAYONNAISE

Serve this spicy mayonnaise with North Carolina Shrimp Boil, or other seafood dishes.

Preparation Time: 20 minutes
Yield: approximately 1½ cups

INGREDIENTS

2 large red peppers, roasted and peeled
or 1 4oz jar roasted pimentos
1 clove garlic, crushed
2 egg yolks
¼ tsp coarse salt
½ tsp fresh tarragon, finely chopped
1 tsp fresh basil, finely chopped
1 tsp flat leaf parsley, chopped
¼ cup red wine vinegar
½ cup peanut oil
½ cup olive oil
Tabasco sauce to taste

METHOD

Purée the red peppers in a food processor until smooth, then add the garlic, egg yolks, salt and herbs. Pulse to blend, then add the vinegar. Combine the peanut and olive oils. With the food processor running, add the oils, drop by drop at first, then in a slow, steady stream until the mixture thickens, scraping the sides of the bowl as necessary. Adjust the seasoning, adding more salt, vinegar and Tabasco sauce to taste.

BEN BARKER, FEARRINGTON HOUSE,
CHAPEL HILL, NC

PAN-FRIED PORK CHOPS

The cornmeal coating makes these pork chops crisp and tasty!

Preparation Time: 15 minutes
Cooking Time: approximately 15 minutes
Serves: 4

INGREDIENTS

4 8oz center cut pork loin chops
½ cup all-purpose flour
¼ cup stone-ground cornmeal
½ tsp salt
¼ tsp black pepper, ground
⅛ tsp cayenne pepper
⅛ tsp paprika
Peanut oil for cooking

METHOD

Combine the flour, cornmeal and spices and dredge the pork chops in this seasoned mixture until they are coated. Heat a cast-iron or other heavy-bottomed frying pan over a medium high heat for 3 minutes, then brush the pan with a thin film of peanut oil. When the oil just smokes, add the coated pork chops and reduce the heat to medium. Cook for 4 minutes, then turn the chops. Cover the pan and cook for a further 4 to 5 minutes, or until the meat is juicy, but no longer pink at the bone.

To serve, place a large spoonful of Apple Rhubarb Sauce onto a warm plate. Arrange a pork chop on top of the sauce and pour additional sauce on top.

BEN BARKER, FEARRINGTON HOUSE,
CHAPEL HILL, NC

APPLE RHUBARB SAUCE

Apple rhubarb makes a refreshing change from the apple sauce so often served with pork.

Preparation Time: 20 minutes
Cooking Time: 15-20 minutes
Serves: 4

INGREDIENTS

4 Granny Smith, Pippin or other tart cooking apples, peeled, cored and cut into ¼-inch slices
4 stalks of young red rhubarb, washed and thinly sliced
1 cup fruity red wine
⅛ cup sugar
3 whole cloves
1 2-inch cinnamon stick
3 allspice berries
Lemon juice to taste

METHOD

Dice the slices from ½ of one apple, cover with water to which you have added some lemon juice and set aside. Combine the remaining apple slices, the rhubarb, wine, sugar and spices in a heavy-bottomed pan and bring to a boil. Simmer until most of the liquid is evaporated. Remove the whole spices and coarsely purée the cooked fruit in a food processor, or by putting it through the medium blade of a food mill. Drain the reserved apple and combine with the purée. Adjust the seasoning with more lemon juice or sugar. The sauce should be fruity, yet tart.

BEN BARKER, FEARRINGTON HOUSE,
CHAPEL HILL, NC

BLACK-EYED PEAS VINAIGRETTE

These delicious black-eyed peas were developed to serve with pan roasted quail, but they are too good to restrict to that use. Why not try serving them with other poultry dishes?

Facing page: Pan-Fried Pork Chops.

NORTH CAROLINA

Preparation Time: 25 minutes
Cooking Time: 20-30 minutes
Serves: 4-6

INGREDIENTS

¼ lb bacon, cut into ¼-inch strips
3oz onions, coarsely chopped
2oz green bell pepper, coarsely chopped
2oz celery, coarsely chopped
3 cloves garlic, finely chopped
½ tsp cayenne pepper
½ tsp black pepper
¼ tsp white pepper
¼ tsp ground cumin
½ tsp dried basil
¼ tsp dried oregano
1 bay leaf
¾ lb fresh black-eyed peas, shelled
or 1 12oz package frozen black-eyed peas
1½ quarts chicken stock, or more if needed
Salt to taste

VINAIGRETTE

¼ cup cider vinegar
¼ cup olive oil
4 scallions, chopped
¼ cup flat-leafed parsley, chopped

METHOD

Fry the bacon in a large skillet until crisp. Remove the bacon and set aside. Cook the onion, pepper and celery in the bacon fat over a medium heat until they are softened. Increase the heat, add the garlic, herbs and spices and stir and cook for 1 minute. Stir in the black-eyed peas with ¾ quart of stock and bring to the boil. Reduce the heat and simmer the peas until they are tender but firm, adding more stock as needed. When the peas are cooked the liquid should be nearly absorbed. Transfer the black-eyed peas to a large bowl and keep warm. Meanwhile, prepare the vinaigrette by combining the vinegar, oil, scallions and parsley. Toss the peas in the vinaigrette, stir in the reserved bacon, season to taste with salt and allow to cool to room temperature before serving.

BEN BARKER, FEARRINGTON HOUSE,
CHAPEL HILL, NC

Trout in Brown Butter with Pecans and Mint.

TROUT IN BROWN BUTTER WITH PECANS AND MINT

Browned butter with lemon, pecans and mint is used to complement crispy fried fresh trout – a winning combination.

Preparation Time: 20 minutes
Cooking Time: approximately 30 minutes
Serves: 4

INGREDIENTS

4 whole rainbow trout, 8-10oz each
2 cups milk
½ cup fresh lemon juice
1 cup all-purpose flour
½ cup stone-ground yellow cornmeal
2 tbsp Kosher salt
1 tsp black pepper, coarsely ground
½ tsp paprika

BROWN BUTTER SAUCE

½lb butter, softened
1½ cups pecans, coarsely chopped
¼ cup lemon juice
¼ cup spearmint leaves, chopped

TO FRY
Peanut oil

GARNISH
Mint sprigs
Lemon crowns

METHOD

To cook the trout, first rinse them under cold water, then soak them, refrigerated, for 2 hours in a mixture of the milk and the lemon juice. Meanwhile, combine the flour, cornmeal, salt, pepper and paprika. Remove the trout from the marinade, drain and roll them in the seasoned flour mixture. It is easiest to cook the trout in two batches. Heat a small amount of peanut oil in a large skillet over a high heat until it is nearly smoking. Carefully place two of the trout in the pan and reduce the heat to medium high. Cook for 4 minutes before turning, then reduce the heat to medium. Cook for a further 3-4 minutes, or until the trout tests done at the backbone. Cook the remaining trout in the same way. When cooked, arrange the fish on individual plates or on a large platter.

To prepare the Brown Butter Sauce, melt the softened butter in an 8-inch skillet over a high heat. Add the pecans and cook until the butter begins to darken and the nuts start to brown. When the butter ceases to foam and clarifies, carefully add ¼ cup lemon juice and the chopped mint leaves. Pour the sauce over the cooked trout and garnish with a lemon crown and a mint sprig.

BEN BARKER, FEARRINGTON HOUSE,
CHAPEL HILL, NC

CRAB CAKES WITH RED PEPPER AND TOMATO SAUCE

The addition of peppers and herbs makes these crab cakes especially tasty.

Preparation Time: 15 minutes
Cooking Time: 10-15 minutes
Serves: 4 as an appetizer

INGREDIENTS

1lb crab meat, picked over for shell particles
2 tbsps red bell pepper, finely chopped
2 tbsps yellow bell pepper, finely chopped
2 tbsps green bell pepper, finely chopped
2 tbsps celery, finely chopped
1 green onion, minced
2 eggs
¼ cup dried bread crumbs
1 tbsp fresh lemon thyme, chopped
1 tbsp flat leaf parsley, chopped
1½ tsps coarse salt
¼ tsp fresh ground pepper
Zest of one lemon, grated

TO COOK
Clarified butter

TO SERVE
Sprigs of lemon thyme
Corn kernels

METHOD

Combine all the ingredients, except for the lemon thyme sprigs and the corn kernels, in a large bowl and mix well. Form the mixture into cakes 1½ inches in diameter and ½ inch thick. Sauté in clarified butter over medium heat for approximately one minute on each side, or until the cakes are lightly browned.

To serve, place a spoonful of Red Pepper and Tomato Sauce on each plate. Arrange several crab cakes on top and garnish with sprigs of lemon thyme and kernels of corn.

BEN BARKER, FEARRINGTON HOUSE,
CHAPEL HILL, NC

RED PEPPER AND TOMATO SAUCE

Serve this flavorful sauce with crab cakes or other seafood.

Preparation Time: 20 minutes
Cooking Time: 10-15 minutes
Serves: 4

INGREDIENTS

4 plum tomatoes, peeled, seeded and coarsely chopped
3 red bell peppers, roasted, peeled, seeded and coarsely chopped
1 tbsp tomato paste
3 tbsps lemon thyme, chopped
Salt to taste
Pepper to taste
Tabasco sauce to taste
Lemon juice to taste

GARNISH

1 ear Silver Queen corn, or other white variety, shucked and removed from the cob

METHOD

Combine the tomatoes and peppers in a heavy-bottomed saucepan. Simmer over medium-low heat until they are very soft. Purée in a food processor, or pass through the fine blade of a food mill. Stir in the tomato paste and leave to cool. When cool, add the lemon thyme and season with salt, pepper, Tabasco sauce and lemon juice to taste. Garnish the sauce with corn kernels which have been blanched in boiling salted water for 15 seconds, then drained and refreshed in cold water.

BEN BARKER, FEARRINGTON HOUSE,
CHAPEL HILL, NC

Above: Crab Cakes with Red Pepper and Tomato Sauce.

CHOCOLATE MINT TORTE WITH BOURBON CRÈME ANGLAISE

This rich and elegant torte makes the perfect ending to a very special meal.

Preparation Time: 1½ hours
Cooking Time: approximately 2 hours
Serves: 12

INGREDIENTS

TORTE
10oz semi-sweet chocolate
5oz unsalted butter
7 eggs, separated

1 cup sugar
⅓ cup white crème de menthe liqueur
1 tsp pure mint extract
¼ tsp salt

GANACHE TOPPING

½ cup heavy cream
4oz semi-sweet chocolate, cut into small pieces

CRÈME ANGLAISE

2 cups light cream or 2 cups half and half
or 1 cup heavy cream + 1 cup milk
7 egg yolks
¾ cup sugar
3 tbsps bourbon

METHOD

To prepare the torte, melt the chocolate and butter in a double boiler, then set aside to cool slightly. In a large bowl, beat the egg yolks with ¾ cup of the sugar until very thick and light. Add the cooled chocolate mixture, the crème de menthe and the mint extract and stir until just mixed. In a separate bowl beat the egg whites with the remaining ¼ cup of sugar and the salt until they form soft peaks. Quickly, but gently, fold the egg whites into the chocolate mixture. Pour the batter into a buttered and floured 10-inch spring-form pan, the bottom of which has been lined with parchment paper. Bake at 300°F for 1 hour, followed by 30 minutes at 250°F. Remove the cake from the oven and immediately run a sharp knife around the sides of the pan to prevent the top of the cake from cracking. Place the pan on a wire rack and allow the torte to cool completely before removing the sides of the pan.

While the torte is cooling, prepare the ganache topping. Heat the cream in a small, heavy-bottomed saucepan over a low heat. Add the chocolate pieces and stir constantly until the chocolate is completely melted. Remove the pan from the heat and place it in an ice bath. Cool, stirring constantly, until the mixture is thickened, but still spreadable. Spread the ganache evenly over the top of the cooled cake. Chill the torte briefly to set the topping.

To prepare the Bourbon Crème Anglaise, beat the egg yolks with ½ cup of the sugar until thick and light. Heat the light cream with ¼ cup of the sugar. Add a little bit of the hot cream to the egg yolks to prevent them from curdling, then gradually add the yolk mixture to the hot cream in the saucepan. Cook over low heat, stirring constantly until the mixture thickens and coats the back of a spoon. Add the bourbon, then strain the Crème Anglaise into a storage container. Chill in the refrigerator until needed.

To serve the torte, cut with a thin-bladed knife which has

been warmed, and clean the knife between each cut. Serve the torte at room temperature with the chilled Bourbon Crème Anglaise.

TORTE RECIPE ADAPTED FROM MAIDA HEATLER "BOOK OF GREAT CHOCOLATE DESSERTS" BY FEARRINGTON HOUSE, CHAPEL HILL, NC

STRAWBERRY RASPBERRY SHORTCAKES

Strawberries and raspberries make a rich and delicious combination in this elegant shortcake recipe.

Preparation Time: 30 minutes
Cooking Time: 10-12 minutes
Serves: 8

INGREDIENTS

SHORTCAKES

3 cups all-purpose flour
1½ tbsps baking powder
¾ tsp salt
¼ cup plus 2 tbsps sugar
Zest of 1 orange, finely grated
1 tbsps orange juice
7 tbsps butter at room temperature, cut into small pieces
½ cup milk
6 tbsps heavy cream

FILLING

1 pint fresh strawberries, sliced
1 pint fresh raspberries
Sugar to taste

METHOD

Combine the flour, baking powder, salt, sugar, orange zest and juice in a mixing bowl. Cut in the butter, then add the milk and cream and stir lightly until the mixture forms a dough which is thick but not sticky. Roll out the dough to a ½-inch thickness on a lightly floured surface. Cut into 3 ½-inch rounds with a biscuit cutter and place on a parchment-lined baking sheet. Bake at 375°F for 10−12 minutes, or until the tops are golden brown.

To prepare the filling, combine the strawberries and raspberries, sprinkle on sugar to taste and leave to stand for

several hours to allow the juices to be drawn out. To assemble, cut each shortcake in half, lightly butter and toast. Cool slightly, then soak the shortcake halves in the collected berry liquid. Place 8 of the halves on plates, cover each with a large spoonful of the berry mixture, allowing some of the berries to cascade onto the plate. Top the berries with a generous spoonful of Champagne Sabayon and cover with the remaining shortcake halves.

KAREN BARKER, FEARRINGTON HOUSE,
CHAPEL HILL, NC

CHAMPAGNE SABAYON

Serve over Strawberry Raspberry Shortcakes, or wherever a special and elegant topping is called for.

Preparation Time: 15 minutes
Cooking Time: approximately 20 minutes
Yield: approximately 1½ cups

Above: Strawberry Raspberry Shortcakes.

INGREDIENTS

6 egg yolks
½ cup champagne
7 tbsps sugar
1 cup heavy cream

METHOD

Combine the egg yolks, champagne and sugar in a large mixing bowl. Place the bowl over a pot of simmering water and whisk constantly until the mixture becomes very thick. The mixture should be just below the boil. Be very careful not to overcook or the eggs will curdle. Remove from the heat and allow to cool to room temperature. Whip the cream to medium peaks and fold into the cooled champagne mixture. Chill until needed.

KAREN BARKER, FEARRINGTON HOUSE,
CHAPEL HILL, NC

VIRGINIA

Virginia, the Old Dominion State, encompasses several distinct landscapes, ranging from the Tidewater to the mountains of the Appalachian Plateau. The Tidewater extends eastwards from Fredricksburg and Richmond. It is bordered by the rich land of the Piedmont − rolling hills planted with tobacco where Thomas Jefferson made his home. Farther west is the Appalachian Plateau and, in the southwest corner on the Kentucky border, the Cumberland Gap, through which settlers passed to reach the rugged lands of the western frontier.

The state of Virginia is officially a Commonwealth, and Virginians often consider themselves to be the aristocrats of the South; when Virginians feel like boasting about their past, they can begin with such names as George Washington, Thomas Jefferson, Robert E. Lee, and Patrick Henry. With its long and illustrious past, Virginia is unique in the South because it reached its peak of prosperity before the American Revolution. At one time, Virginia and its territories encompassed all of Britain's claims to North America. Settlement of the Dominion began when James I of England chartered two companies to establish colonies in North America. The first to succeed was the London Company, which founded Jamestown in 1607. Under the leadership of John Smith and with the help of the local Indians, the first permanent English settlement was formed.

Facing page: Grey's Hill Roast Turkey with Cornbread Stuffing. Above: Parke's Salamagundi.

METHOD

Arrange the meat and fish in a circular pattern on a large serving platter. Surround with the celery hearts, salad greens and pickles. Pour a light coating of French dressing over all just before serving.

WOODLAWN PLANTATION COOK BOOK,
JOAN SMITH, EDITOR,
MOUNT VERNON, VA

Preparation Time: 30 minutes
Serves: 6-8

INGREDIENTS

1lb Virginia ham, julienned
1lb chicken or turkey, julienned
6 hard-boiled eggs, sliced
8oz anchovy fillets
4oz sardines in olive oil
Assorted pickles
Celery hearts
Assorted salad greens
1 cup or more of your favorite French dressing

GREY'S HILL ROAST TURKEY WITH CORNBREAD STUFFING

A stuffed holiday bird with a definite Southern accent.

I N G R E D I E N T S

CORNBREAD STUFFING

2 tbsps butter
½ cup chopped onion
2 tbsps chopped celery
2 tbsps green pepper
2 cups corn bread cubes
1 cup bread cubes
1 tbsp chopped parsley
Salt to taste
Pinch thyme
½ cup or more chicken stock or water

ROAST TURKEY

10-12lb turkey at room temperature
2 tsps baking soda
2 tsps salt
1 tsp pepper
2 tbsps butter, softened
4 tbsps butter, melted
½ cup cognac

M E T H O D

First prepare the stuffing. Melt the butter and sauté the onion, pepper and celery until tender. Stir in the remaining stuffing ingredients and moisten with chicken stock or hot water.

Preheat the oven to 450°F. Wash and dry the turkey. Rub the inside of the body and neck with salt, baking soda and pepper. Lightly stuff the cavities with the cornbread stuffing and sew or skewer closed. Tuck the wings under and fasten the legs down. Rub the surface of the bird with the softened butter and place on a rack in a shallow baking pan, breast side up. Combine the melted butter and cognac to use as a baste. Place the turkey in the preheated oven and immediately reduce the heat to 325°F. Roast uncovered for 1 hour, basting frequently. Make a loose tent out of aluminum foil and lay on top of the bird. Continue cooking for a further 3 hours, basting from time to time. If you run out of the baste, pour some boiling water into the bottom of the roasting pan, stir up the drippings and use this liquid as a baste. Remove the foil during the last 30 minutes to allow the bird to brown. The turkey is done when the leg joint moves freely. Remove from the oven and allow the bird to stand for 20 minutes before carving.

RIDGEWELL CATERER, INC.
WOODLAWN PLANTATION COOK BOOK,
JOAN SMITH, EDITOR,
MOUNT VERNON, VA

ANGELA'S CORN PUDDING

This is one of many recipes for an old Virginia favorite. You can serve it for a light meal on its own, or use it as an accompaniment to meat.

Preparation Time: 15 minutes
Cooking Time: 1 hour
Serves: 4-6

I N G R E D I E N T S

3 eggs
¼ cup flour
1 tsp salt
½ tsp white pepper
2 cups fresh cut corn or 2 cups frozen corn,
thawed and drained
2 tbsps butter, melted
2 cups half and half

M E T H O D

Preheat the oven to 325°F. Beat the eggs vigorously and add the flour, salt and pepper. Blend well, then stir in the corn, melted butter and half and half. Pour the batter into a buttered 1½-quart soufflé dish or casserole. Place the dish in a pan of hot water and bake for 1 hour, or until a knife inserted in the center comes out dry.

WOODLAWN PLANTATION COOK BOOK,
JOAN SMITH, EDITOR,
MOUNT VERNON, VA

LORENZO'S COUNTRY HAM

Preparation Time: 15 minutes
Soaking Time: 12 hours or more
Cooking Time: 12 hours or overnight
Serves: 3 per lb

I N G R E D I E N T S

1 whole country ham, uncooked
4 cups water
½ cup sugar
1 cup fine dry bread crumbs

Above: Smoked Tuna Salad.

TO COOK
Heavy duty aluminum foil

METHOD

Soak the ham for 12 hours or longer. Wash thoroughly and scrub off all of the mold. Preheat the oven to 400°F. Place the ham on a large sheet of heavy duty aluminum foil and put in a roasting pan. Join the sides of the foil to form a container. Pour in the water and seal the top of the foil. Roast for 20 minutes, then turn off the oven for 3 hours, leaving the ham inside and the oven door closed. Reheat the oven to 400°F and, when it has come up to temperature, roast for a further 20 minutes. Turn off the oven again and leave the ham inside for 6-8 hours or overnight. Do not open the oven door during the entire cooking cycle. When the cooking time is up, remove the ham from the foil and, while still warm, carefully remove the skin and all but a very thin layer of the fat. Sprinkle the ham with the sugar and bread crumbs and bake, uncovered, at 400°F for 15 minutes, or until the ham is nicely browned. Cool and slice as thinly as possible to serve.

Leftover ham can be stored in the refrigerator, wrapped in foil or plastic for 3 weeks or more. Eternity has been defined as two people and a ham, but you will find any leftover ham so delicious in casseroles and soups that you will wish it could last for ever!

WOODLAWN PLANTATION COOK BOOK,
JOAN SMITH, EDITOR,
MOUNT VERNON, VA

SMOKED TUNA SALAD

This makes an elegant and delicious luncheon salad. If you don't have champagne vinegar, try using a herb vinegar instead.

VIRGINIA

Preparation Time: 15 minutes
Marinating Time: 1-2 hours
Serves: 4-6

INGREDIENTS

8oz smoked tuna
8oz can artichoke hearts, drained and quartered
½ red pepper, thinly sliced
4 leaves fresh basil, finely chopped
3 scallions, sliced
1 tomato, diced
¼ cup Extra Virgin olive oil, or more to taste
⅛ cup champagne vinegar, or more to taste

TO SERVE

Fresh salad greens

METHOD

Combine the artichoke hearts, pepper, basil, scallions and tomato. Toss lightly with the olive oil. Season with salt and pepper and gently toss again with the champagne vinegar. Allow the mixture to marinate for 1-2 hours before adding the smoked tuna. Toss lightly to combine and serve on a bed of fresh salad greens.

SUSAN PAINTER,
THE SHIP'S CABIN SEAFOOD RESTAURANT,
NORFOLK, VA

GRILLED SEAFOOD BROCHETTES

Use the freshest seafood you can find to make these colorful brochettes. They make wonderful fare at a summer barbecue. Serve with boiled rice and a sauce of hot lemon caper butter.

Preparation Time: 30 minutes
Cooking Time: 10 minutes
Serves: 6

INGREDIENTS

3 lemons, cut into quarters
9oz salmon, cut into 6 pieces
3 small tomatoes, cut into quarters

Grilled Seafood Brochettes.

12 large shrimp
3 small green peppers, cut into quarters
9oz swordfish, cut into 6 pieces
6 large mushrooms
12 large scallops
3 6oz lobster tails, cut in half
Vegetable oil

METHOD

Coat 6 skewers with a small amount of vegetable oil to prevent sticking and divide the seafood and vegetables among the

Above: Nelly Custis' Maids of Honor. Facing page: Joan Smith's Thanksgiving Pie.

skewers. Make sure that you place the skewers through the center of the pieces. Grill over a hot charcoal for 5-10 minutes, or until the ingredients are tender.

JOE HOGGARD,
THE SHIP'S CABIN SEAFOOD RESTAURANT,
NORFOLK, VA

NELLY CUSTIS' MAIDS OF HONOR

These popular treats originally came from England, but were very popular in early America.

Preparation Time: 20 minutes
Cooking Time: 45 minutes
Yield: 8-10 tarts

INGREDIENTS

Pastry to line 8-10 3½-inch tart pans
2 eggs
½ cup sugar
½ cup almond paste
1-2 tbsps sherry
2 tbsps melted butter
1 tbsp lemon juice
2 tbsps flour
8-10 tsps strawberry or raspberry jam

METHOD

Preheat the oven to 350°F. Use the pastry to line the tart pans and arrange them on a baking sheet. Beat the eggs until very light and fluffy. Gradually beat in the sugar. Soften the almond paste with the sherry, butter and lemon juice. Add this mixture to the beaten eggs. Drop 1 teaspoon of jam into each tart shell and fill with the batter. Bake for about 45 minutes, or until puffed, golden and firm.

RIDGEWELL CATERER, INC.
WOODLAWN PLANTATION COOK BOOK,
JOAN SMITH, EDITOR,
MOUNT VERNON, VA

JOAN SMITH'S THANKSGIVING PIE

Try this marvellous version of pumpkin pie for your next holiday feast.

Preparation Time: 1 hour
Cooking Time: 1 hour and 15 minutes
Serves: 6-8

INGREDIENTS

NUT MERINGUE SHELL

½ cup walnuts or pecans, ground
3 egg whites
¼ tsp cream of tartar
⅛ tsp salt
1 cup sugar
½ tsp cinnamon

PUMPKIN CHIFFON FILLING

1 cup walnuts or pecans, ground
1 tbsp plain gelatine
¼ cup sherry or dark rum
⅔ cup brown sugar, packed
½ tsp salt
1 tsp cinnamon
½ tsp nutmeg
½ tsp ginger
3 eggs, separated
¾ cup milk
1 cup cooked puréed pumpkin
⅓ cup sugar

TOPPING

1 cup heavy cream
1 tbsp sugar
¼ cup dark rum

METHOD

To prepare the meringue shell, first preheat the oven to 275°F. Beat the egg whites with the cream of tartar and salt until they form soft peaks. Gradually add the sugar, about 2 tablespoons at a time, until the meringue stands up in stiff, glossy peaks. Beat in the cinnamon along with the last ¼ cup of sugar. Gently fold in the nuts. Pile the meringue onto a lightly-greased 9-inch pie plate. Spread it over the bottom to approximately ¼-inch thickness and up the sides to form a crust. Bake for 50-60 minutes until the shell is a light tan color. Turn off the oven and leave the meringue to cool with the door closed. The meringue will crack and fall in the center. When the meringue is cool, press the center lightly to make a shell.

Facing page: Apple Torte.

To prepare the filling, soften the gelatine in the sherry or rum. Combine with the brown sugar, salt, spices, beaten egg yolks and milk. Cook and stir over a low heat until the mixture thickens, about 10 minutes. Remove from the heat and stir in the pumpkin. Chill until the mixture is very thick. Meanwhile, beat the egg whites to soft peaks and gradually beat in the sugar to form a meringue. Fold the meringue into the pumpkin mixture along with ⅔ cup of the nuts. Spoon the filling into the cooled meringue shell and sprinkle the remaining nuts around the edge. Chill until firm.

To prepare the topping, beat the cream to soft peaks, add the sugar and stir in the rum. Add a large spoonfull to each serving of pie.

RIDGEWELL CATERER, INC.
WOODLAWN PLANTATION COOK BOOK,
JOAN SMITH, EDITOR,
MOUNT VERNON, VA

APPLE TORTE

Serve this delicious dessert warm or cold with vanilla ice cream.

Preparation Time: 20 minutes
Cooking Time: 45 minutes
Serves: 6-8

INGREDIENTS

⅔ cup flour, sifted
3 tsps baking powder
½ tsp salt
2 eggs, beaten
1½ cups sugar
3 tsps vanilla
2 cups apples, peeled, cored and diced
1 cup pecans or walnuts, chopped

METHOD

Preheat the oven to 350°F. Sift together the flour, baking powder and salt. Set aside. In a separate bowl, combine the sugar, vanilla and beaten eggs. Stir in the dry ingredients, apples and nuts. Pour the batter into a buttered 8x12x4-inch baking dish. Bake for 45 minutes or until a knife inserted in the center comes out clean.

RIDGEWELL CATERER, INC.
WOODLAWN PLANTATION COOK BOOK,
JOAN SMITH, EDITOR,
MOUNT VERNON, VA

KENTUCKY

When the first settlers entered Kentucky through the Cumberland Gap in 1750, they found a land of great beauty. The area that was to become known as the Bluegrass State of Kentucky or, in the words of the native Wyandot Indians, the Land of Tomorrow, is a land of contrasts. The western part of the state, bordered by the Ohio and Mississippi rivers, is dominated by the enormous Kentucky Lake and Lake Barkley. South central Kentucky is on a limestone terrain and is well known for its many magnificent caves, including the spectacular Mammoth Cave. Perhaps the most famous region in Kentucky is the Bluegrass, which extends from the mountains in the east to the Ohio River in the west and centers around Lexington. The area is noted for its rich soils, which produce lush grass and tobacco and high-quality horseflesh. The Eastern Highlands, around the Cumberland Gap, which were once better known for mountain moonshine and feuding families, are now more visited for the beauty of their mountains, forests, gorges, and waterfalls.

Kentucky is Daniel Boone country. Abraham Lincoln, the 16th President of the United States, and Jefferson Davis, the president of the Confederacy, were both born in the state. Kentuckians are proud of their past, and the state contains many carefully restored monuments to its famous sons.

KENTUCKY

The Old South is alive and well in Kentucky, where a gracious and leisurely pace is still valued. "Settin' out" is a favorite way to relax on a hot afternoon, and farming families gather at noon for dinner with all the "fixin's." Religion and family life are what binds the people together. Fundamentalist Christianity is very strong here and central Kentucky is punctuated with small, beautifully tended churches.

One Christian sect that made its way to Kentucky were the Shakers, an offshoot of the English Quakers who came to America in 1774, just before the outbreak of the American Revolution. They gathered thousands of converts to their "Kingdoms of God upon Earth." The brothers and sisters established communities where the only rule for living was the Golden Rule. They would gather daily to pray and dance both for pure joy for the countless gifts the Lord had bestowed upon them, and in order to drive away any wrong thoughts or desires. The Shakers listened for the still, small voice and turned to God for inspiration, guidance, and revelation in every facet of their lives.

The Shaker sisters believed that the planning and preparation of meals was an important responsibility and a great service to God. They took up the task of providing three meals a day for all their members, as well as any travelers who cared to stop, with joy and practicality. Their cooking was characterized by its careful preparation, imaginative use of herbs and vegetables, and high quality. The Shaker's wasted nothing, and developed methods for handling large amounts of food using exact weights and measures in a time when most people relied on a handful of this and a dash of that to reproduce recipes. Some of the earliest American cookbooks were produced by the Shakers. They also pioneered the art of preserving as they developed numerous types of pickles and relishes in order to store the summer harvests for the long winters. Because Shaker communities also served as orphanages, many young girls were trained by the Shakers to conduct well-run and thrifty homes. Thus the influence of the Brethren who "gave their hands to work and their hearts to God" was considerable.

A group of Shakers founded a communal religious colony in Kentucky at Pleasant Hill, twenty-two miles southwest of Lexington, in 1805. The spirit of the Shaker kitchens lives on, and you can sample some of their favorite recipes in this small collection, gathered at Pleasant Hill.

Facing page: Shaker Lemon Pie.

TOMATO CELERY SOUP

The addition of the fresh vegetables makes canned tomato soup taste homemade.

Preparation Time: 15 minutes
Cooking Time: 5 minutes
Serves: 4

INGREDIENTS

1 small onion, chopped
½ cup finely chopped celery
2 tbsps butter
1 10½oz can of tomato soup
1 can water
1 tsp chopped parsley
1 tbsp lemon juice
1 tsp sugar
¼ tsp salt
⅛ tsp pepper

GARNISH

¼ cup unsweetened cream, whipped
Chopped parsley

METHOD

Sauté the onion and celery in the butter, but do not brown. Add the tomato soup, water, parsley, lemon juice, sugar, salt and pepper. Simmer for 5 minutes. The celery will remain crisp. To serve, pour into 4 bowls and top each with a spoonful of unsweetened whipped cream and a sprinkling of chopped parsley.

COURTESY ELIZABETH C. KREMER
FROM THE TRUSTEES HOUSE DAILY
FARE, PLEASANT HILL, KENTUCKY
PLEASANT HILL PRESS, HARRODSBURG,
KENTUCKY 1970 AND 1977

CHICKEN CROQUETTES

This is a delicious and economical way to use up leftover chicken. Try serving the croquettes with Mushroom Cream Sauce.

Preparation Time: 30 minutes
Cooking Time: 2-4 minutes each
Serves: 8-12

INGREDIENTS

2 cups dry bread crumbs
1½ cups chicken broth
4 cups cooked chicken
1 cup mushrooms
1 tsp chopped onion
½ cup chopped celery
½ tsp salt
⅛ tsp red pepper
1 tbsp chopped parsley
Dash lemon juice

TO FRY

1 cup dry bread crumbs
1 beaten egg
2 tbsps water or milk

METHOD

Soak the bread crumbs in the broth. Meanwhile, grind together the chicken and mushrooms, Combine with the soaked bread crumbs and the rest of the ingredients and allow to cool. Shape into 24 croquettes and chill. To cook, dip each croquette into dry bread crumbs, then into a mixture of beaten egg and water or milk, and finally into bread crumbs again. (This is the secret of good croquettes!) Fry in deep fat, heated to around 375°F, or until a 1 inch cube of bread browns in 1 minute, until golden (approximately 2-4 minutes).

COURTESY ELIZABETH C. KREMER
FROM THE TRUSTEES HOUSE DAILY
FARE, PLEASANT HILL, KENTUCKY
PLEASANT HILL PRESS, HARRODSBURG,
KENTUCKY 1970 AND 1977

MUSHROOM CREAM SAUCE

This creamy sauce is a perfect partner for Chicken Croquettes, but you can use it in other ways too. Try it with fresh vegetables or over scrambled eggs on toast for a quick and delicious supper.

Preparation Time: 10 minutes
Cooking Time: 15 minutes
Yield: approximately 3 cups

INGREDIENTS

3 tbsps butter
¼ cup flour
1½ cups warm milk
1½ cups canned unsweetened condensed milk
1 cup sliced fresh mushrooms
1 tbsp butter
Dash paprika
Salt and pepper to taste

METHOD

Melt the butter in the top of a double boiler. Whisk in the flour, pepper, salt and paprika until well blended and smooth. Add the milk and condensed milk slowly, stirring constantly to prevent lumps. Continue to cook and stir until the sauce is smooth and thick. Lightly brown the sliced mushrooms in 1 tablespoon of butter and stir into the sauce. Add the paprika, salt and pepper to taste.

COURTESY ELIZABETH C. KREMER
FROM THE TRUSTEES HOUSE DAILY
FARE, PLEASANT HILL, KENTUCKY
PLEASANT HILL PRESS, HARRODSBURG,
KENTUCKY 1970 AND 1977

Above: Tomato Celery Soup.

BISQUE OF GARDEN PEAS

When those peas start coming in from the garden, this is a delicious way to add variety to your menu.

Preparation Time: 20 minutes
Cooking Time: 15-20 minutes
Serves: 4

INGREDIENTS

3 cups peas, fresh or frozen
2 cups water
¼ cup onions, chopped
3 tbsps butter
3 tbsps all-purpose flour
3 cups milk or half and half
Salt and red pepper to taste

METHOD

Cook the fresh peas in water with a pinch of salt until tender. If using frozen peas, follow the directions on the package.

Cool slightly then combine the peas, water and onions and purée. Melt the butter in a large saucepan and stir in the flour until smooth and bubbly. Remove from the heat and stir in the milk slowly. Return to low heat and cook, stirring constantly, until the sauce thickens. Add the puréed pea mixture and stir until well blended. Season to taste with red pepper and salt. Serve chilled, garnished with fresh mint leaves.

COURTESY ELIZABETH C. KREMER
FROM THE TRUSTEES HOUSE DAILY
FARE, PLEASANT HILL, KENTUCKY
PLEASANT HILL PRESS, HARRODSBURG,
KENTUCKY 1970 AND 1977

KENTUCKY COUNTRY HAM

Country ham is sugar cured, smoked and hung for up to 18 months to develop its full flavor. Don't worry about the exterior mold. It is harmless and is scrubbed off before cooking.

Preparation Time: 30 minutes
Cooking Time: 1 hour 20 minutes, plus 20 minutes per lb
Serves: 3-4 people per lb

INGREDIENTS

1 country ham
½ cup whole cloves
1 cup brown sugar
1 cup vinegar
1½ gallons water
GLAZE
1 cup brown sugar
1 cup cornmeal
1 tbsp ground cloves
1 tsp cinnamon

METHOD

Scrub the ham well to remove the exterior mold and soak overnight in the water. Sprinkle half of the cloves into the bottom of a roasting tin, place the ham on top, and sprinkle the remaining cloves on top of the ham. Bake for 1 hour at 375°F, then reduce the temperature to 275°F and cook for 20 minutes per pound, or until an internal temperature of 150°F is reached. When the ham is fully cooked, remove from the roasting tin, trim if necessary and bone if desired. Wash the roasting tin and replace the cooked ham. Prepare the glaze by combining the brown sugar, cornmeal and spices. Sprinkle this mixture over the ham and brown in the oven at 375°F until the glaze has melted.

COURTESY ELIZABETH C. KREMER
FROM THE TRUSTEES HOUSE DAILY
FARE, PLEASANT HILL, KENTUCKY
PLEASANT HILL PRESS, HARRODSBURG,
KENTUCKY 1970 AND 1977

PLEASANT HILL BAKED EGGPLANT

The creamy filling makes an attractive contrast against the brilliant purple of the eggplants. You could substitute summer squash for the eggplant if you wish.

Preparation Time: 30 minutes

Cooking Time: 30-35 minutes
Serves: 4-6

INGREDIENTS

1 large eggplant
FILLING
½ medium onion, chopped
3 tbsps butter
3 tbsps chopped parsley
1 10½oz can cream of mushroom soup
1-2 cups unsalted butter crackers, crushed
Dash of Worcestershire sauce
Salt and pepper to taste

METHOD

Cut off the top of the eggplant and scrape out the inside, leaving about ½ inch around the sides and bottom of the shell. Boil the eggplant flesh in salted water until tender. Drain well and chop. Sauté the chopped onion in 2 tablespoons butter and add the parsley. Mix in the cooked eggplant, soup and seasonings. Add enough cracker crumbs to make a good stuffing consistency. Pile the mixture into the eggplant shell, sprinkle with cracker crumbs and dot with the remaining tablespoon of butter. Bake at 375°F for 30-35 minutes, or until the eggplant is soft.

COURTESY ELIZABETH C. KREMER
FROM THE TRUSTEES HOUSE DAILY
FARE, PLEASANT HILL, KENTUCKY
PLEASANT HILL PRESS, HARRODSBURG,
KENTUCKY 1970 AND 1977

SCALLOPED OYSTER PLANT

The oyster plant, also known as salsify, is a root vegetable with a delicate oyster-like flavor.

Preparation Time: 30 minutes
Cooking Time: 30 minutes
Serves: 4-6

Facing page: Chicken Croquettes.

INGREDIENTS

1 large oyster plant
2 cups bread or cracker crumbs
2 tbsps butter
1 cup cream

TOPPING

1 cup bread crumbs
4 tbsps butter

METHOD

Slice the oyster plant into water to which you have added a little vinegar in order to prevent discoloration. Drain, then cook in fresh boiling water until tender and drain well. Arrange alternate layers of cooked oyster plant and cracker crumbs in a greased baking dish, beginning with a cracker crumb layer and ending with a layer of oyster plant. Dot each layer with butter and seasonings. Pour over the cream.

To prepare the topping, melt the butter in a saucepan and stir in the bread crumbs. Spread this mixture on top of the layers and bake at 400°F for approximately 30 minutes, or until the liquid is absorbed.

COURTESY ELIZABETH C. KREMER
FROM THE TRUSTEES HOUSE DAILY
FARE, PLEASANT HILL, KENTUCKY
PLEASANT HILL PRESS, HARRODSBURG,
KENTUCKY 1970 AND 1977

CORN STICKS

All the secrets of good corn bread are revealed in this recipe!

Preparation Time: 10 minutes
Cooking Time: 10 minutes
Yield: approximately 12 sticks

INGREDIENTS

1 cup + 2 tbsps cornmeal
½ cup flour
3 tsps sugar
½ tsp baking soda
½ tsp baking powder
½ tsp salt
2 tbsps oil
1 cup buttermilk
1 egg

METHOD

Mix together the dry ingredients, then beat in the oil, egg and buttermilk. One of the secrets of good corn bread is to beat very well. Heat greased irons until hot enough to sizzle (this is the other secret of making good corn bread) and fill to half full. Bake at 450°F for about 10 minutes, or until brown.

COURTESY ELIZABETH C. KREMER FROM
THE TRUSTEES HOUSE DAILY
FARE, PLEASANT HILL, KENTUCKY,
PLEASANT HILL PRESS, HARRODSBURG,
KENTUCKY 1970 AND 1977

SHAKER LEMON PIE

This tart and refreshing pie is unusual in that it uses the whole lemon, not just the juice.

Preparation Time: 30 minutes plus standing time
Cooking Time: 35 minutes
Serves: 6-8

INGREDIENTS

PASTRY

2 cups all-purpose flour
1 tsp salt
⅓ cup shortening
⅓ cup butter, chilled
5 tbsps cold water

FILLING

2 large lemons
4 eggs, well beaten
2 cups sugar

METHOD

To prepare the pastry, combine the butter and salt in a bowl. Cut in the shortening and butter until the mixture resembles coarse bread crumbs. Gradually sprinkle on the cold water and blend lightly with a fork, until you can just gather the dough into a ball. Divide the dough into 2 pieces and leave to rest in a cool place for at least ½ hour. Roll out one of the pieces and line a 9-inch pie plate. Roll out the second piece to form a top crust.

To make the filling, wash the lemons and slice them paper thin, rind and all. Cover with the sugar and let stand for at least two hours, overnight is better, stirring occasionally. Add

Pleasant Hill Baked Eggplant and Kentucky Country Ham (left), Scalloped Oyster Plant (center and right) and Corn Sticks (top).

to 375°F and bake for about 20 minutes or until a knife inserted near the edge of the pie comes out clean. Cool before serving.

the beaten eggs and mix well. Turn the filling into the lined pie dish. Cover with the top crust and cut several slits near the center. Bake at 450°F for 15 minutes, then reduce heat

COURTESY ELIZABETH C. KREMER
FROM THE TRUSTEES HOUSE DAILY
FARE, PLEASANT HILL, KENTUCKY
PLEASANT HILL PRESS, HARRODSBURG,
KENTUCKY 1970 AND 1977

TENNESSEE

Tennessee, the land beyond the mountains, the wild frontier of colonial America, combines many of the virtues of the past with the realities of life in the twentieth century. The rugged pioneers who settled here were people of grit and determination. In the Mexican war of 1846, when Tennessee was asked for 2,800 men, 30,000 volunteered. Ever since then it has been nicknamed the Volunteer State. The Civil War left the state cruelly divided. Tennessee was the last to leave the Union and the first to rejoin. In spite of its Yankee leanings, Tennessee retains many of the good old-fashioned Southern virtues of loyalty and love of place.

Although it clings to the past, the state is quickly moving into the present. Memphis now challenges Atlanta as the medical research center of the southeast, and Nashville is the "third" coast of the music industry—a place where hundreds of hopefuls gather to wait for their big break.

The state is divided into three distinct areas. The mountainous east is the hickory-smoked paradise of Appalachia; conservative, down-home, and remembered for hillbillies and moonshine. Middle Tennessee is a pleasantly tolerant place of gentle people who cling to the old virtues. Limestone, which filters the water for the Jack Daniel's Distillery in Lynchburg, underlies much of this region of rolling hills, horse farms, and the man-made reservoirs of the

Tennessee Valley Authority. In contrast, the flat western part of the state remains firmly rooted in the agricultural traditions of the Deep South.

Southern traditions dominate the cuisine of the state. Grits and vegetables such as greens, black-eyed peas, and squash are popular. Pork, much of it home-produced, is prepared in many ways. Some Tennesseans who hold down full-time jobs cling to their rural heritage by doing a little hog farming on the side. Hog killing time is the time to taste golden-brown fried chitlins made from the small intestines of the hogs. Home-made sausage recipes are passed down through the generations and the ribs are saved for barbecuing over hickory smoke.

Barbecues are a favorite summer occupation in Tennessee, as they are in many parts of America. Cooking over an open fire is an ancient art, but, since colonial days, it has become an American tradition. The word barbecue was first used in the colony of Virginia in the late seventeenth century to describe spit roasting. It is said to have come from the phrase *de barbe à queue* (from beard to tail), borrowed from the French-speaking Louisiana settlers. It developed into an important social form in the early nineteenth century, a friendly gathering of friends and neighbors.

Spare ribs, barbecued over hickory charcoal and basted with a tasty sweet-and-sour sauce, are favorites at a Tennessee barbecue. Fried fresh corn and corn light bread, made up the night before and allowed to stand overnight to "sour" before baking, are traditional accompaniments, all washed down with Lynchburg Lemonade (for adults only!).

And for dessert — well, besides the luscious pies and cakes made ahead, there is home-made ice cream, frozen in a hand-cranked churn, then wrapped in old quilts and left to "ripen" for a few hours to bring out the flavor. If you've got the urge to sample some of these down-home delights, you'll find these and other recipes in this collection from cooks in Nashville, Murfreesboro, Lynchburg, and Springfield. You'll never leave the table hungry!

Facing page: Brunch Cheese Grits (left) and Brunch Scrambled Eggs (right).

BRUNCH CHEESE GRITS

These tasty cheese-flavored grits are sure to find a place on
your next brunch table.

Preparation Time: 20 minutes
Cooking Time: 1 hour
Serves: 4-6

INGREDIENTS

3 cups boiling salted water
¾ cup quick-cooking grits
⅓ cup butter or margarine, softened
½lb sharp Cheddar cheese, grated
⅛ tsp Tabasco sauce
1 tbsp onion, finely grated (optional)
2 eggs, beaten
½ tsp Worcestershire sauce
1½ tsps seasoning salt or
½ tsp each garlic salt, paprika and onion salt

METHOD

Stir the grits into the boiling water and cook for 3 minutes.
Remove from the heat and mix in the remaining ingredients.
Blend well. Pour the batter into a 2-quart greased casserole.
Bake, uncovered, at 250°F for 55 to 60 minutes, or until a
silver knife or cake tester inserted in the center comes out
clean. Serve hot.

DORIS BELCHER, MEMPHIS, TN

BRUNCH SCRAMBLED EGGS

A dash of paprika makes a pretty garnish for these delicious
scrambled eggs. They go nicely with Brunch Cheese Grits.

Preparation Time: 10 minutes
Cooking Time: 10 minutes
Serves: 4-6

An appetizing Tennessee brunch spread, including
Brunch Cheese Grits, Brunch Scrambled Eggs, Squash
Side Dish, Angel Biscuits and Good Morning Coffee
Cake.

Above: Squash Side Dish.

INGREDIENTS

2 tbsps butter
6 eggs, slightly beaten
¾ cup cottage cheese, drained
2 tbsps milk or cream
1 tbsp chives, chopped
Pinch marjoram leaves
Pinch cayenne pepper
½ tsp salt

METHOD

Gently mix together the eggs, cottage cheese, milk and seasonings. Melt the butter over a low heat in a heavy skillet. Add the egg mixture and cook slowly, turning the mixture with a spatula when it begins to thicken.

DORIS BELCHER, MEMPHIS, TN

SQUASH SIDE DISH

Preparation Time: 20 minutes
Cooking Time: 15 minutes
Serves: 8

INGREDIENTS

3 tbsps butter
1 medium onion, chopped
1 medium bell pepper, diced
2 medium zucchini squash, sliced
2 medium yellow summer squash, sliced

14½oz can tomato wedges
½ tsp garlic salt
Salt and pepper to taste

GARNISH

Fresh parsley
Grated Parmesan cheese

METHOD

Melt the butter in a heavy skillet, add the onion and cook until transparent. Stir in the bell pepper and continue cooking until soft. Add the squash and seasonings, cover, and simmer until just tender. Drain the tomatoes, reserving the liquid, and add them to the skillet. Cook for an additional 5 to 8 minutes, adding some of the reserved liquid if needed.

Garnish this colorful dish with parsley and sprinkle with Parmesan cheese before serving.

DORIS BELCHER, MEMPHIS, TN

ANGEL BISCUITS

Angel biscuits are like their name—heavenly!

Preparation Time: 20 minutes
Cooking Time: 10-12 minutes
Yield: approximately 50 biscuits

INGREDIENTS

5 cups all-purpose flour
1 tsp baking powder
1 tsp salt
¾ cup vegetable shortening
2 cups milk
2 tbsps sugar
1 package yeast (about 1oz)
½ cup warm water

METHOD

Sift together the flour, baking powder and salt and cut in the shortening with two knives or a pastry cutter until the mixture resembles coarse bread crumbs. Dissolve the yeast in the warm water and stir in the sugar. Add the yeast along with the milk to the dry ingredients and stir until the mixture is moist. To make biscuits, roll the dough onto a floured surface to a ½-inch thickness. Cut with a biscuit cutter and bake on greased baking sheets. Bake at 400°F for 10-12 minutes, or

until the biscuits are lightly browned. If you prefer, the dough may be stored, covered, in the refrigerator for up to one week and baked as needed.

DORIS BELCHER, MEMPHIS, TN

BLOODY MARY COCKTAIL

Pour these spicy Bloody Marys over cracked ice in tall glasses for a delicious, refreshing reviver.

Preparation Time: 5 minutes
Serves: 8

INGREDIENTS

1 46oz can V-8 or tomato juice (or a mixture of the two)
8-10oz vodka
9 tbsps Worcestershire sauce
2-3 dashes Tabasco sauce
1 tbsp prepared horseradish
1 tbsp dried parsley (optional)
¾ tsp celery salt
Juice of 2 lemons

METHOD

Mix the ingredients together in a large glass jar and chill. Stir well before serving.

DORIS BELCHER, MEMPHIS, TN

GOOD MORNING COFFEE CAKE

If you know this coffee cake is waiting, getting up should be no problem.

Preparation Time: 20 minutes
Cooking Time: 25-30 minutes
Yield: 8-inch-square cake

INGREDIENTS

1½ cups self-rising flour or 1½ cups all-purpose flour,
½ tsp salt and 2 tsps baking powder
½ cup sugar
1 egg, beaten

½ cup milk
3 tbsps vegetable oil

STREUSEL TOPPING

¼ cup flour
¼ cup sugar
½ tsp cinnamon
2 tbsps butter
2 red apples, unpeeled and cut into eighths

M E T·H·O D

To make the cake, sift together the flour and sugar. In a separate bowl, mix the egg, milk and oil. Gradually add this liquid to the dry ingredients, stirring until the batter is smooth. Pour the mixture into a greased 8-inch square or a 9-inch round pan. Set aside while you prepare the Streusel Topping. To make the topping, combine the flour, sugar and cinnamon in a bowl. Cut in the butter until the mixture resembles coarse crumbs. Sprinkle over the batter and arrange the apple slices in a circle on top. Bake at 400°F for 25-30 minutes or until a knife inserted in the center comes out clean. Serve hot.

DORIS BELCHER, MEMPHIS, TN

TENNESSEE FRIED CORN

Use really fresh corn to obtain the full flavor of this delicious dish.

Preparation Time: 30 minutes
Cooking Time: 20 minutes
Serves: 4

I N G R E D I E N T S

2 cups fresh corn (6-8 ears)
5 tbsps butter and bacon drippings, mixed
1 tsp sugar
1-1½ cups water
Salt and pepper to taste

M E T H O D

Select corn which has full, round, milky kernels. Remove the shucks and the silk. Run a sharp knife along the ears to cut off the tips of the kernels, then scrape the edge of the knife along the cob to remove all of the milky portion which remains. Heat the fat in a heavy skillet. Add the corn, water, sugar, salt and pepper. Stir constantly to heat through. Lower

the heat and cook, stirring frequently, until the corn is thickened and almost transparent in color. This will take about 15-20 minutes.

CALLIE LILLIE OWEN,
COURTESY *NASHVILLE COOKBOOK*

MARINATED CUCUMBERS

Preparation Time: 20 minutes
Serves: 8

I N G R E D I E N T S

4 cucumbers, sliced
1 small onion, thinly sliced
¼ cup sugar
⅔ cup vinegar
½ tsp celery seed
1½ tsps salt

M E T H O D

Combine the cucumber and onion slices. Sprinkle with the salt and sugar, then add the vinegar and celery seed. Mix thoroughly to combine. Cover and chill until ready to serve.

Garnish this crisp, cool salad with slivers of red radishes for a lovely summery contrast.

PAT COKER, NASHVILLE, TN

TENNESSEE RIBS

The long cooking over hickory charcoal and the frequent basting with the sweet sauce make these ribs something special.

Preparation Time: 20 minutes
Cooking Time: approximately 2 hours
Serves: 6

I N G R E D I E N T S

4-5lbs spare ribs

SAUCE

8oz can tomato sauce
½ cup sherry

½ cup honey
2 tbsps wine vinegar
2 tbsps onion, minced
1 clove garlic, minced
¼ tsp Worcestershire sauce

M E T H O D

Arrange the ribs in a shallow roasting pan and bake at 350°F for 30 minutes. Meanwhile, in a saucepan, combine the sauce ingredients and simmer for 5 minutes. Prepare a fire in a barbecue using hickory charcoal. Push the coals to one side of the grill and, when the coals are ashed over, place the ribs on the part of the grill which is away from the coals. Grill indirectly in this way for about 45 minutes, then move the ribs directly over the coals. Brush them frequently with the sauce as you continue to grill them for a further 20-30 minutes.

MARY ANN FOWLKES, NASHVILLE, TN

CORN LIGHT BREAD

Corn light bread is traditionally served at barbecues in mid-Tennessee. In the "olden days" corn light bread was made up at night and allowed to stand overnight to "sour." It was baked early in the morning for the noon and evening meals. This quick version can be stored wrapped and served several days after baking, or frozen for later use.

Preparation Time: 20 minutes
Cooking Time: 25 minutes
Yield: 1 loaf

Below: Angel Biscuits and Good Morning Coffee Cake.

INGREDIENTS

1 cup cornmeal
1 cup flour
½ cup sugar
½ tsp salt
2 tsps baking powder
1 egg, beaten
1¼ cups buttermilk
1 tbsp shortening, melted or
1 tbsp cooking oil

METHOD

Preheat the oven to 400°F. Grease a loaf pan and heat. Combine the dry ingredients in a mixing bowl. In a separate bowl, mix together the egg and buttermilk, then add the melted shortening. Stir the liquid mixture into the dry ingredients until combined. Pour the batter into the loaf pan and bake for about 25 minutes, or until done.

MARY STANFILL,
COURTESY OF *NASHVILLE COOKBOOK*

CUSTARD VANILLA ICE CREAM

Preparation Time: 20 minutes
Cooking Time: 10 minutes
Chilling time: at least 3 hours
Yield: 1 gallon

INGREDIENTS

1 cup sugar
1½ tbsps flour
½ gallon milk, scalded
½ pint whipping cream
6 eggs, beaten
14oz can sweetened condensed milk
1 tbsp vanilla
6 Goo Goo Clusters, crumbled
or chocolate peanut candies

A mouthwatering spread featuring as its main dish Tennessee Ribs.

METHOD

Combine the flour and sugar in a heavy saucepan. Gradually stir in the scalded milk and the whipping cream. Cook over a medium heat, stirring constantly until thickened, then continue to cook for a further 2 minutes. Remove from the heat and add the condensed milk and vanilla. Chill for at least two hours, then fold in the crumbled Goo Goo Clusters. Freeze the mixture in a 1-gallon ice cream freezer according to the manufacturer's instructions.

If you can bear to wait, this ice cream has the best flavor if allowed to "ripen" or stand for 2 hours before serving. To do this, pack the ice cream freezer with additional ice and salt, then insulate with covers of newspaper or old quilts.

ANN COX, MURFREESBORO, TN

CHOCOLATE CREAM PIE

Don't expect any leftovers when you serve this irresistible creation!

Preparation Time: 45 minutes
Cooking Time: 25 minutes
Serves: 1 9-inch pie

INGREDIENTS

1 pre-baked 9-inch pie shell
1 cup sugar
¼ cup cocoa
¼ cup cornstarch
¼ tsp salt
3 cups milk
3 egg yolks
1 tsp vanilla extract

MERINGUE TOPPING

3 egg whites
½ tsp vanilla
¼ tsp cream of tartar
6 tbsps sugar

Barbecue Chicken, accompanied by All-American Potato Salad, American Baked Beans, Triple Bean Salad Piquant and Curry Dip, with a selection of vegetables, makes a memorable 4th of July picnic.

METHOD

To prepare the filling, combine the sugar, cocoa, cornstarch and salt in a heavy saucepan. Mix together the milk and egg yolks and gradually stir into the sugar mixture. Cook over a medium heat, stirring constantly, until the mixture thickens and boils. Continue to cook and stir for 1 minute, then remove from the heat and add the vanilla. Pour the hot filling into the pre-baked pie shell. To make the topping, beat the egg whites and the cream of tartar at room temperature using an electric mixer at high speed. Add the sugar, a tablespoon at a time, and continue to beat until stiff peaks form and the sugar is dissolved. Spread the meringue over the hot filling right to the edge of the pastry to form a seal. Bake at 350°F for 12-15 minutes, or until the meringue is golden brown. Cool before serving.

ELSIE WALKER, SPRINGFIELD, TN

BARBECUE CHICKEN

Here is a delicious alternative to Southern Fried Chicken.

Preparation Time: 20 minutes
Cooking Time: 1 hour 20 minutes
Serves: 4

INGREDIENTS

1 fryer chicken (about 2½lbs), cut into pieces
½ cup flour
Salt and pepper

SAUCE

1 medium onion, chopped
2 tbsps vegetable oil
2 tbsps vinegar
2 tbsps brown sugar
¼ cup lemon juice
1 cup ketchup
3 tbsps Worcestershire sauce
½ tbsp prepared mustard
1 cup water
Dash Tabasco sauce

METHOD

Shake the chicken pieces in a paper bag containing the flour, salt and pepper. Brown in a heavy skillet using a small amount of vegetable oil. Drain off any excess oil and place the chicken in a shallow baking pan. Set aside while you prepare the sauce. To make the sauce, brown the onion in the vegetable oil in a heavy skillet. Add the remaining sauce ingredients and simmer for 20 minutes. Pour the sauce over the chicken and bake, uncovered, at 325°F for 1 hour, or until the chicken is tender. Baste frequently with the sauce during the cooking time.

DORIS BELCHER, MEMPHIS, TN

ALL-AMERICAN POTATO SALAD

Here is a delicious salad to serve with the Triple Bean Salad Piquant for a gorgeous summer meal.

Preparation Time: 15 minutes
Cooking Time: 2 hours or more
Serves: 8

INGREDIENTS

4 cups diced cold boiled potatoes
1-2 tbsps minced onion
¼ cup celery, chopped (optional)
2 tbsps chopped pimento
½ cup mayonnaise
¼ cup chopped dill pickle
½ tsp prepared mustard
½ tsp salt
Pepper to taste
2-3 hard-boiled eggs, coarsely chopped

METHOD

Combine all the ingredients except for the eggs, and toss carefully until well mixed. Add the eggs, reserving some for a garnish, and mix gently. Garnish the salad with the reserved eggs and chill for at least 2 hours before serving.

DORIS BELCHER, MEMPHIS, TN

TRIPLE BEAN SALAD PIQUANT

This super salad is so easy to make, and sure to please!

Preparation Time: 10 minutes

Cooking Time: 8 hours or overnight
Serves: 8-10

INGREDIENTS

1 16oz can wax beans, drained
1 16oz can cut green beans, drained
1 16oz can dark red large kidney beans, drained
½ cup sliced celery
1 medium bell pepper, deseeded and diced
1 medium sweet onion, sliced into rings
½ cup sugar
½ cup salad oil
¾ cup cider or wine vinegar

METHOD

Toss the vegetables together in a large salad bowl. Combine the sugar, oil and vinegar and pour over the vegetables. Allow to marinate, refrigerated, for 8 hours or overnight. Toss the vegetables to distribute the dressing before serving.

DORIS BELCHER, MEMPHIS, TN

AMERICAN BAKED BEANS

Long, slow cooking gives these baked beans a succulent flavor.

Preparation Time: 15 minutes
Cooking Time: 9½ hours
Serves: 6-8

INGREDIENTS

2 cups dried navy, pea or southern white beans
½lb salt pork, diced
¼ cup diced onion
3 tbsps molasses
¼ tsp dry mustard
2 tsps salt
Pinch pepper

GARNISH

4 strips of bacon (optional)

METHOD

Cover the beans with cold water and leave to soak for 8 hours. Simmer in the soaking water until they are barely tender, about

1½ hours. Drain and reserve the liquid. Place the beans, pork and onion in a greased baking dish. Combine the molasses and the seasonings and pour over. Cover and bake at 275°F for about 8 hours. Check several times during the cooking and add the reserved liquid if the dish seems dry. Remove the cover for the last 4 hours. If desired, place the strips of bacon over the top during the last half of the cooking time.

DORIS BELCHER, MEMPHIS, TN

CURRY DIP

Serve this tasty dip with a selection of raw vegetables such as carrot and celery sticks, sliced squash, and broccoli flowerets.

Preparation Time: 10 minutes

Above: Triple Bean Salad Piquant.

Cooking Time: overnight
Yield: approximately 2 cups

INGREDIENTS

1 cup mayonnaise
3oz cream cheese, softened
1 tsp tarragon vinegar
½ tsp prepared horseradish
½ tsp garlic salt
1 tsp curry powder

METHOD

Combine all the ingredients and chill the dip in the refrigerator overnight. If the dip is too stiff, add a small amount of milk to soften.

DORIS BELCHER, MEMPHIS, TN

PICKLED OKRA

With this tasty pickle in your store cupboard you will always have a crunchy snack ready to serve to unexpected guests.

Preparation Time: 30 minutes
Cooking Time: 10 minutes
Yields: approximately 6 pints

INGREDIENTS

3 cups white vinegar
3 cups water
1½ cups sugar

6 cloves garlic
5lbs small to medium okra, trimmed
Salt (non-iodized)

METHOD

To prepare the okra for pickling, remove the stem and trim the top of the pod. Pack the okra and garlic into sterilized pint jars. Combine the vinegar, water and sugar in a saucepan and bring to the boil. Pour over the okra and add ½ tsp salt to each pint. Seal the jars and process for 10 minutes in a boiling water bath.

DORIS BELCHER, MEMPHIS, TN

FRESH FRUIT COBBLER

Serve this tempting dessert warm with cream or whipped cream. You can vary the fruit to suit the season.

Preparation Time: 30 minutes
Cooking Time: 30 minutes
Serves: 6-8

INGREDIENTS

¾-1 cup sugar
1 tbsp cornstarch
1 cup water
3½ cups sliced fresh fruit (for example apples, peaches or berries, plus juice)
½ tbsp butter
Pinch cinnamon

PASTRY

1 cup all-purpose flour
⅓ tsp salt
⅓ cup plus 1 tbsp shortening
2-3 tbsps cold water
½ tbsp butter, melted
Pinch cinnamon

METHOD

Combine the sugar, cornstarch and water and bring to a boil. Boil for 1 minute, then add the fruit and juice and cook for a further minute. Pour into a well buttered 1½-quart baking dish. Sprinkle lightly with the cinnamon and dot with the butter. Prepare the pastry by combining the flour and salt. Cut in the shortening until the mixture resembles coarse crumbs. Sprinkle in the water and mix gently until the dough can be formed into a soft ball. Roll out on a floured surface to a ⅛-inch thickness. Cut the dough into ½-inch-wide strips and arrange in a lattice pattern over the fruit. Brush the pastry with melted butter, sprinkle with cinnamon and bake at 400°F for 30 minutes, or until the cobbler is golden brown and bubbly.

DORIS BELCHER, MEMPHIS, TN

LYNCHBURG LEMONADE

Serve this refreshing cooler on a hot summer's day.

Preparation Time: 5 minutes
Serves: 8-12

INGREDIENTS

¾ cup Jack Daniel's whiskey
¾ cup Triple Sec liqueur
¾ cup sweet and sour mix
1 ¾ cups 7-UP

METHOD

Combine all the ingredients in a pitcher. Add plenty of ice and garnish with lemon slices and maraschino cherries.

JACK DANIEL'S DISTILLERY,
LYNCHBURG, TN

Facing page: Curry Dip with Pickled Okra and a selection of fresh vegetables. Below: Fresh Fruit Cobbler.

ALABAMA

Alabama, originally the home of the Five Nations—the Cherokee, Seminole, Muscogee, Chickasaw, and Chocktaw Indians—was called the land of the thicket clearers by the Chocktaws. But it was the European settlers who first tamed the wilderness and brought agriculture and industry to the region.

The first Europeans to arrive in Alabama were the Spanish colonists, who landed near Mobile on the Gulf Coast in 1559. Alabama was settled by the French and was part of the British colony of West Florida before becoming the twenty-second state in the Union in 1819. At the outbreak of the Civil War, Alabama joined the Confederacy. Although the war was lost, the pride and glory of the Confederate era survives in Alabama, especially in the capital, Montgomery, which was the first capital of the Confederate States. Many descendants of Confederate soldiers from Alabama are as genuinely proud of their ancestors' fight for independence against the United States as Bostonians are of their fight against the British.

ALABAMA

The culinary influence of the early European settlers is felt mostly along the Gulf Coast, where fish and seafood dishes with a strong French accent are served. The early French influence can also be seen in the fact that winegrowing was once a great domestic industry in Alabama. The wine industry, stifled in the early twentieth century under prohibition, has been revived in a small way in the area east of Mobile. But instead of the famous grape varieties of the French vineyards, the wine grapes grown here include Scuppernongs, Higgins, Nobles, and Magnolias. Away from the coast, real Southern home cooking—fried chicken, green beans, yellow squash, okra, and especially biscuits—is the staple.

If there is one thing guaranteed to make a Southerner feel at home, it is fresh biscuits at every meal. Now, as in the early days, biscuits are popular because they are so quick to make. The basic recipes are simple, but there is more to biscuit making than simply following a recipe and this is a skill best learned from an experienced Southern cook.

There are many types of biscuits, ranging from the thin baking powder biscuits which often accompany meals, to the thick, fluffy shortcakes, split and served with fruit and whipped cream. Some biscuits are enriched with mashed sweet potatoes or cheese and red peppers, but the trickiest of all to make are the beaten biscuits. No leavening agent is used in these and their texture depends entirely on the long working of the dough. The dough must be beaten with a mallet, or put through the coarse chopper of a meat grinder and folded over frequently. This kneading process requires at least half an hour and a good deal of strength. In plantation kitchens the cooks gave the dough 200 licks for the home folks, but 500 if they expected company.

This collection of recipes, gathered in Montgomery and Selma, will give you plenty of chances to try your hand at reproducing the proud traditions of the Southern kitchen. The past may be gone, but it is certainly not forgotten in Alabama, as Alabama's cooks will be happy to remind you.

Facing page: Southern-Style Potato Soup.

ALABAMA

SOUTHERN-STYLE POTATO SOUP

Makes a refreshing soup on a hot day.

Preparation Time: 30 minutes, plus chilling
Cooking Time: approximately 50 minutes
Yield: 1½ quarts

INGREDIENTS

1½ cups green onions, white part only, diced
½ cup onions, chopped
1 tbsp butter
3 cups baking potatoes, peeled and diced
3 cups hot water
3 tsps salt
1 cup hot milk
½ tsp white pepper
1 cup light cream
1 cup heavy cream
8 tsps chopped chives

METHOD

In a heavy 4-quart pot, sauté the onions in the butter until soft, but not brown. Add the potatoes, hot water and 2 tsps of the salt. Simmer, uncovered, for 30-40 minutes, or until the potatoes are soft. Liquidize the potatoes and onions, and return to the pot. Add the hot milk, and slowly bring the soup to a boil, stirring often to keep the potatoes from settling. Add the remaining salt and the pepper. Remove from the heat and strain through a sieve. Cool the soup, stir, then strain again and add the light and heavy cream. Serve chilled and garnished with the chopped chives.

STURDIVANT MUSEUM ASSOCIATION,
SELMA, AL

MARINADED PORK LOIN WITH ORANGE SAUCE

The orange adds a refreshing tang to a succulent pork roast.

Preparation Time: 30 minutes
Cooking Time: 2½ hours
Serves: 8

INGREDIENTS

5lb loin of pork or
8 pork chops, 1 inch thick

MARINADE
½ cup lemon juice
½ cup soy sauce
½ cup red wine
½ tsp pressed garlic
2 tsps ground ginger

ORANGE SAUCE
⅔ cup sugar
½ tsp cinnamon
1 tblsp grated orange rind
20 whole cloves, tied in a cheesecloth bag
1 tbsp cornstarch
½ tsp salt
1 cup orange juice
8 orange slices, cut into halves

METHOD

Combine the marinade ingredients and pour over the pork. Cover and refrigerate overnight, turning occasionally. Remove the meat, reserving the marinade for basting. Roast at 350°F, basting often with the reserved marinade, for approximately 2½ hours, or until the meat registers 185°F on a meat thermometer. To prepare the orange sauce, combine the sugar, spices, orange rind, orange juice, cornstarch and salt in a saucepan and cook over a medium heat, stirring frequently, until the sauce is thickened and clear. Remove the bag of cloves and add the orange slices.

To serve, arrange the meat on a serving platter and pour the orange sauce over the meat.

STURDIVANT MUSEUM ASSOCIATION,
SELMA, AL

SWEET POTATO BISCUITS

Biscuits are a way of life in the South. Here is a version which uses sweet potatoes as a basis.

Facing page: Butter Bean Salad (left), Marinaded Pork Loin with Orange Sauce (center) and Southern Fried Chicken (right).

Preparation Time: 30 minutes
Cooking Time: 10-12 minutes
Yield: approximately 4 dozen

INGREDIENTS

3 cups flour
½ tsp baking soda
2 tsps baking powder
3 tbsps shortening
3 cups cooked sweet potatoes, mashed
1 cup buttermilk
Pinch salt
Sugar, if necessary

METHOD

Sift together the dry ingredients and cut in the shortening. In a separate bowl, combine the mashed sweet potatoes and salt. Taste, and add sugar by teaspoonsful until the flavor blossoms. Stir the buttermilk into the sweet potatoes and add to the dry ingredients. Mix together quickly with a fork. Turn the dough out onto a lightly floured board. Knead until the dough is no longer sticky, adding as little extra flour as possible. Roll out to a ½-inch thickness and cut with a biscuit cutter. Bake at 450°F for 10-12 minutes, or until lightly browned. Serve hot with butter or hard sauce.

CREATIVE CATERERS,
MONTGOMERY, AL

BUTTER BEAN SALAD

This salad is a delicious alternative to a mixed green salad, and could form the basis of a light luncheon when served with fresh, hot biscuits.

Preparation Time: 15 minutes
Cooking Time: 40 minutes
Serves: 8

INGREDIENTS

30oz fresh or frozen butter beans
4 cups water
1 tsp salt

Butter Bean Salad.

4 hard-boiled eggs, chopped
1 small onion, finely grated
1 cup mayonnaise
¾ tsp prepared mustard
¾ tsp Worcestershire sauce
¾ tsp hot sauce

METHOD

Boil the butter beans in the water and salt for 40 minutes. Drain, then combine with the rest of the ingredients. Refrigerate the salad overnight and serve on a bed of lettuce.

STURDIVANT MUSEUM ASSOCIATION,
SELMA, AL

SOUTHERN FRIED CHICKEN

This is one way to cook that real Southern Fried Chicken!

Preparation Time: 15 minutes
Cooking Time: 30 minutes
Serves: 4

INGREDIENTS

1 chicken, fresh or killed the day before
Flour for dredging
Salt and pepper to taste

METHOD

Cut the chicken into portions and wipe dry. Dredge in flour which has been seasoned with salt and pepper. Fry in boiling oil in a skillet. Cook only a few pieces at a time.

STURDIVANT MUSEUM ASSOCIATION,
SELMA, AL

CHEESE BISCUITS

These are a flavorful variation on the biscuit theme.

Preparation Time: 15 minutes
Cooking Time: 10 minutes
Yield: 24

INGREDIENTS

1 cup sharp cheese, grated
1 cup flour
1 tsp baking powder
½ tsp salt
½ tsp red pepper
1 tsp butter
1-2 tbsps cold water

METHOD

Combine the dry ingredients and rub in the butter. Stir in enough water to make a stiff dough. Roll out on a lightly floured surface to about ½-inch thickness and cut into small biscuits. Bake at 450°F for 10 minutes, or until browned.

STURDIVANT MUSEUM ASSOCIATION,
SELMA, AL

SHORT BISCUITS

Preparation Time: 20 minutes
Cooking Time: 10-15 minutes
Yield: approximately 2 dozen

INGREDIENTS

1¼ cups flour
½ tsp salt
1 tsp baking powder
1 tbsp shortening
5 tbsps or more cold water

METHOD

Preheat the oven to 350°F. Sift together the dry ingredients and cut in the shortening. Stir in the water to form a stiff dough. Roll out on a floured board to a ½-inch thickness and cut with a small biscuit cutter. Bake for 10-15 minutes, or until light brown on top.

STURDIVANT MUSEUM ASSOCIATION,
SELMA, AL

Facing page: Southern Fried Chicken.

CHICKEN COUNTRY CAPTAIN

Legend has it that a sea-captain brought this recipe back from India, but whatever its origin, it will certainly become a favorite in your house.

Preparation Time: 45 minutes (including frying)
Cooking Time: 2 hours
Serves: 6

INGREDIENTS

¼ cup vegetable oil
1½ cups chopped onions
¾ cup chopped green pepper
1 clove garlic, minced
1 32-oz can tomatoes, drained and chopped
1 tsp curry powder
¼ tsp thyme
⅛ tsp cayenne pepper
2 tbsps chopped parsley
4lb frying chicken, cut into serving-size pieces
1 cup flour, seasoned with salt and pepper
½ cup water
½ cup currants
32 whole roasted almonds

TO SERVE

3 cups cooked rice

METHOD

Sauté the onions, garlic, green pepper and curry powder in the oil until the vegetables are tender. Add the thyme, cayenne, parsley and tomatoes. Cover, and simmer for 1 hour over a low heat. Meanwhile, sprinkle the chicken pieces with salt and pepper and dredge in the seasoned flour. Fry the pieces until just done, about 10-15 minutes, in deep fat which has been heated to 375°F, or until a 1-inch cube of bread browns in 1 minute. Place the cooked chicken in a roasting pan, add the water and sprinkle with the currants. Pour the simmered vegetables over, cover tightly and bake at 325°F for 1 hour.

Garnish with the roasted almonds and serve over very hot cooked rice.

CECIL L. McMILLAN, THE ONCE IN A
BLUE MOON COOKBOOK

Chicken Country Captain and Baked Stuffed Yellow Squash (main dish) and Turnip Greens.

TURNIP GREENS

Try these greens, which are familiar fare throughout the South.

Preparation Time: 15 minutes
Cooking Time: 45 minutes
Serves: 4

INGREDIENTS

2oz lean salt pork
2 cups boiling water
2lbs turnip greens
Salt to taste

METHOD

Rinse the salt pork, score several times and add to the boiling water. Simmer rapidly for 15 minutes. Meanwhile, wash the greens thoroughly and remove any tough stems. Tear into small pieces. Add to the pork, packing into the saucepan if necessary. Cover and simmer over medium heat for 30 minutes, or until the greens are tender. Taste the broth halfway through the cooking time and add salt if necessary.

CREATIVE CATERERS,
MONTGOMERY, AL

BAKED STUFFED YELLOW SQUASH

This is a dish to try in the summer, when squashes are so plentiful and cheap.

Preparation Time: 20 minutes
Cooking Time: 35-40 minutes
Serves: 8

INGREDIENTS

8 medium yellow squash
1 onion, finely chopped
4 tbsps butter
2 tbsps Worcestershire sauce (optional)
½ cup fine bread crumbs
2 egg yolks, beaten
Salt and pepper to taste

METHOD

Cook the unpeeled squash in boiling salted water until it is just tender, about 15 minutes. Cut off the stem end and a ½-inch-thick slice off the top. Carefully scoop out the flesh, leaving the shell intact. Chop the flesh, together with the top slice, and drain well. Melt the butter in a heavy skillet and sauté the onions until they are tender and translucent. Stir in the chopped squash and most of the bread crumbs, reserving some to sprinkle on the top. Season lightly with salt and pepper. Remove the vegetables from the heat, cool slightly, then stir in the beaten egg yolks. Use this mixture to stuff the squash shells. Sprinkle with the reserved bread crumbs, then bake on a greased baking sheet at 350°F for 20-25 minutes.

CECIL L. McMILLAN, THE ONCE IN A
BLUE MOON COOKBOOK

BEATEN BISCUITS

The long beating is the secret to making these biscuits light and tasty.

Preparation Time: 30 minutes
Cooking Time: 15 minutes
Yield: 44

INGREDIENTS

4 cups flour
1 tsp baking powder (optional)
3 tsps salt
½ cup shortening
½ cup ice water

METHOD

Mix together the flour and salt and cut in the shortening. Add enough cold water to make a stiff dough. Beat very well until the dough is smooth; this may take 20 minutes or more. Roll the dough out on a lightly floured surface to a ½-inch thickness and cut with a biscuit cutter. Bake for about 15 minutes in a hot oven (425-450°F).

STURDIVANT MUSEUM ASSOCIATION,
SELMA, AL

Facing page: Turnip Greens.

Above: Charlotte.

BIG MOMMY'S FLOATING ISLAND

Use your imagination to vary the flavorings in this spectacular dessert.

Preparation Time: 30 minutes
Cooking Time: 20-25 minutes
Serves: 8-10

INGREDIENTS

CUSTARD

2 cups whole milk
3 egg yolks or 2 whole eggs
¼ cup sugar
½ tsp vanilla
⅛ tsp salt
A flavoring, such as nutmeg, amaretto or grated orange or lemon peel

"ISLANDS"

3 egg whites
1 tsp cream of tartar
1 tbsp sugar

METHOD

To prepare the custard, scald the milk. Beat the eggs lightly and add the sugar and salt. Add this mixture to the hot milk, stirring constantly. Cook in the top of a double boiler, stirring often, until the mixture thickens and coats the back of the spoon. Cool and flavor using the flavoring of your choice. Chill the custard while you prepare the "Islands". Beat the egg whites and cream of tartar until stiff and gradually beat in the sugar to make a meringue with stiff peaks. Using a large tablespoon, float the meringues onto a roasting pan filled with hot milk or water. Brown in a preheated 400°F oven. Remove from the pan and drain.

Below: Big Mommy's Floating Island.

To assemble the dessert, pour the chilled custard into a serving bowl. Using a slotted spoon, arrange the drained meringues on top.

MRS. JOHN H. NAPIER III

CHARLOTTE

This elegant and delicious dessert will grace any dinner party table.

Preparation Time: 30 minutes
Cooking Time: approximately 10 minutes
Serves: 8-10

INGREDIENTS

2 tbsps unflavored gelatin
¼ cup cold water
2 cups milk
4 eggs, separated
½ cup sugar
⅛ tsp salt
2 tbsps whiskey
1 pint whipping cream
1 dozen lady fingers

METHOD

In a mixing bowl, sprinkle the gelatin over the cold water and leave to soak until all of the gelatin is moist. Heat the milk to just below boiling and set aside to cool slightly. Meanwhile, separate the eggs and beat the yolks slightly. Add the sugar and salt, followed by a small amount of the hot milk. Stir well. Add this mixture to the remaining hot milk and cook over a low heat, stirring constantly, until the mixture coats the back of the spoon. Pour this mixture over the gelatin in the mixing bowl and stir until the gelatin is dissolved. Cool, then add the whiskey. When the mixture begins to gel, beat the egg whites until stiff, but still moist. Fold the egg whites into the custard by cutting a spoon through the egg whites and custard and turning the custard over the egg whites. Blend in this manner until no lumps of egg white are visible. Beat the cream until stiff and fold into the mixture in the same way as the egg whites. Line a mold with lady fingers and spoon the custard mixture on top. Cover and chill thoroughly.

To serve, unmold and top with additional whipped cream.

STURDIVANT MUSEUM ASSOCIATION,
SELMA, AL

JEFFERSON DAVIS PUNCH

This festive punch was especially created by the Davis family to celebrate a family birthday.

Preparation Time: 15 minutes
Yield: 200 cups of punch

INGREDIENTS

1½ pints lemon juice
3½ lbs sugar dissolved in water
12 bottles claret
2 bottles light rum

2 bottles dry sherry
1 bottle ginger ale
6 bottles club soda

GARNISH

Ice
Cucumber slices
Orange slices

METHOD

Combine all the ingredients in a large punch bowl. Dilute with water to taste. Float ice, cucumber and orange slices on top.

DAVIS FAMILY

TOASTED PECANS

These nuts are wonderful served slightly warm on a cold night. They also freeze well for another time.

Preparation Time: 10 minutes
Cooking Time: 10 minutes
Yield: 1lb

INGREDIENTS

1lb pecan halves, shelled
½ stick (2oz) butter
Salt to taste

METHOD

Preheat the oven to 350°F. Melt the butter in a saucepan and add the pecans. Toss with a wooden spoon over a high heat until the butter has been absorbed. Spread the pecans on a cookie sheet and bake for approximately 10 minutes. Watch carefully because the nuts burn easily. When the pecans are bubbly and toasted, remove from the oven and immediately spread them on layers of absorbent paper towels. Sprinkle with salt while still hot. Cool before storing.

MRS. JOHN H. NAPIER III,
HAMNER GARLAND FREEMAN Jr.

Facing page: Jefferson Davis Punch and Toasted Pecans.

MISSISSIPPI

The state of Mississippi is dominated by the great river — called the "Father of the Waters" by the Algonquin Indians — which shares its name. In the northeastern corner of the state the end of the Appalachian foothills provide a terrain of gently rolling hills. Otherwise, from its beautiful coastline along the gulf of Mexico to the fertile plains of the Mississippi delta, the landscape is flat. The flat plains are the home of the great cotton fields, which were the basis of the state's economy.

Traditionally the most conservative of the old Southern States, Mississippi was one of the strongholds of the Confederacy. In this cradle of southern ideals, and home of Jefferson Davis, cotton was king, and Old Man River, the mighty Mississippi, was the lifeline to the outer world. Mississippi represented the South of the lacy white riverboat, the coffee house, moonlight, and magnolias.

MISSISSIPPI

The Spanish explorer Hernando de Soto was the first to reach Mississippi, but it was the French who began settlement in 1699 on the Gulf coast. They eventually reached the great river and established Natchez, once the richest city in the cotton empire and the heartbeat of the southern aristocracy in the late eighteenth century. Farther up river, the French also founded the original settlement at Vicksburg, where the defeat of the Confederacy began. When Vicksburg, the only remaining Confederate stronghold on the Mississippi River, fell after a forty-seven-day seige, the fate of the Confederacy was sealed, although it was two years before Robert E. Lee surrendered at Appomattox Courthouse.

The cuisine of Mississippi reflects the many aspects of its history. Although New Orleans remains the bastion of French influence in America, the influence of the early French settlers can also be seen in the kitchens of Mississippi, especially in the elegant meals served in the beautifully restored ante-bellum mansions along the Mississippi River. Some of these plantation homes can still be visited, and there you can sample the rich sauces and spectacular desserts for which the Creole school of cooking is famous.

The other side of Mississippi cooking is the food of those who consider themselves "just plain folks." The old-style southern breakfast can still be found in some restaurants in the state. Today's abbreviated menu is likely to include two kinds of meat, as well as eggs, hominy grits, hot biscuits, and waffles. In the past you would have been offered fried chicken as well!

For dinner, try catfish, caught in the Mississippi River, served crisp-fried with a tasty cornmeal coating and accompanied by hush puppies. These deep-fried nuggets of cornmeal were originally made from the batter left over from the fresh corn bread served at most meals, which was fried and fed to the dogs to keep them quiet. Another day, taste some slowly simmered turnip greens, flavored with salt pork and served with their pot liquor.

This collection of recipes, gathered around Vicksburg, samples the cooking of all Mississippi, and reflects the fascinating blend of history and the tradition of warm Southern hospitality so characteristic of the Magnolia State.

Facing page: Hot 'n' Spicy Red Beans and Rice, Bourbon Ribs
and Bell Pepper Baked Beans.

EGGS BENEDICT WITH HOLLANDAISE SAUCE

It would be difficult to think of a more elegant breakfast or brunch dish than these carefully prepared eggs.

Preparation Time: 20 minutes
Cooking Time: 10-15 minutes
Serves: 2

INGREDIENTS

HOLLANDAISE SAUCE
¾ cup clarified butter
3 tbsps water
3 egg yolks
Juice of ½ lemon
Salt and white pepper to taste

EGGS BENEDICT
2 poached eggs
2 thick slices of Canadian bacon
2 tbsps sherry
1 English muffin
1 tbsp butter

GARNISH
2 asparagus stems

METHOD

Begin by preparing the Hollandaise sauce. Melt the clarified butter and leave to cool to lukewarm. Meanwhile, in a small, heavy saucepan, whisk the water with the egg yolks and a little salt and pepper for approximately 30 seconds, or until stiff. Place the pan over a low heat and whisk constantly until the mixture is thick and creamy. The pan should be warm, but never hot to the touch. Remove from the heat and stir in the clarified butter, a few drops at a time. When the sauce begins to thicken, the butter may be added a little quicker, but be careful not to add the butter too quickly or the sauce will curdle. When all the butter has been incorporated, stir in the salt, white pepper and lemon juice to taste. Keep warm, but not hot, while you prepare the Eggs Benedict.

Poach the eggs and keep warm in a bowl of warm water. Preheat the oven to 250°F. Place the bacon in a baking dish and pour over the sherry. Cover tightly with foil and place in the oven to warm. Split and toast the muffin and spread with the butter. When the bacon is warmed, place one slice on each muffin half. Drain the eggs and arrange on top of the bacon.

To serve, spoon warm Hollandaise sauce over the eggs and garnish each with an asparagus stem.

CARL ANDRÉ FLOWERS,
CEDAR GROVE ESTATE, VICKSBURG, MS

SHERRY CAKE

Although some commercial mixes are used in the preparation of this cake, the results definitely taste home-made.

Preparation Time: 30 minutes
Cooking Time: 50 minutes
Serves: 10-12

INGREDIENTS

STREUSEL FILLING
⅓ cup brown sugar
¼ cup flour
3 tbsps firm butter or margarine
½ tsp cinnamon
¾ cup toasted almonds

CAKE BATTER
1 18½oz package yellow cake mix
4 large eggs
¾ cup cream sherry
¾ cup vegetable oil
1 3⅝oz package instant vanilla pudding mix
½ tsp nutmeg

SHERRY GLAZE
2 cups sifted powdered sugar
⅓ cup melted butter or margarine
1 tbsp cream sherry
1-2 tbsps hot water

METHOD

Grease and flour a 10-inch Bundt pan and set aside. Prepare the Streusel Filling by rubbing the butter into a mixture of the brown sugar, flour and cinnamon until crumbly. Stir in the toasted almonds and set aside. In a large mixing bowl, combine the cake mix, eggs, sherry, oil, pudding mix and

Facing page: Sherry Cake (left), Blueberry Breakfast Muffins (right) and Eggs Benedict with Hollandaise Sauce (bottom).

nutmeg. Beat by hand for 5 minutes or use an electric mixer for one minute on low speed followed by 3 minutes on medium speed, making sure that you scrape the bowl often. Pour half of the batter into the prepared pan. Sprinkle evenly with the streusel filling, then pour in the remaining batter. Bake at 350°F for 45-50 minutes, or until the cake springs back when touched lightly. Cool on a wire rack for 15 minutes before unmolding, then leave to cool completely. While the cake is cooling, prepare the sherry glaze. Combine all of the glaze ingredients and add enough hot water to produce a glaze thick enough to coat the back of a spoon. When the cake is fully cooled, brush with the sherry glaze and garnish with the toasted almonds.

ANN HALL, GREY OAKS,
VICKSBURG, MS

BLUEBERRY BREAKFAST MUFFINS

Fresh or frozen blackberries can be used instead of blueberries if you wish. Muffins like this make it worth getting up on a cold morning!

Preparation Time: 15 minutes
Cooking Time: 20-25 minutes
Yield: 12

INGREDIENTS

1 egg
½ cup milk
¼ cup vegetable oil
½ cup sugar
1½ cups flour
2 tbsps baking powder
½ tsp salt
1 cup blueberries, fresh or frozen

METHOD

Beat the egg with a fork and stir in the milk and the oil. Combine the dry ingredients and add to the egg mixture, blending just until the flour is moistened. The batter will be lumpy. Carefully stir in the blueberries. Bake in greased muffin tins for 20-25 minutes at 400°F, or until a toothpick inserted in the center of a muffin comes out clean.

FRANCIS M. GIBSON,
CEDAR GROVE ESTATE, VICKSBURG, MS

DATE NUT BREAD

Serve this fragrant bread toasted and buttered, with coffee or tea.

Preparation Time: 15 minutes
Cooking Time: 1 hour
Yield: 1 large loaf

INGREDIENTS

3 eggs
¾ cup vegetable oil
1 8oz package dates, chopped
1 cup hot water
1 cup chopped nuts
2 cups plain flour
2 cups sugar
2 tsps baking powder
1 tsp ground cloves
1 tsp ground allspice
1 tsp cinnamon
½ tsp salt

METHOD

Set the dates to soak in the hot water. Meanwhile, beat the eggs and add the sugar and the oil. Stir in the dry ingredients and mix lightly. Add the nuts and the dates in their soaking water and mix just to combine. Pour the batter into a greased and lined loaf pan. Bake at 325°F for 1 hour, or until a toothpick inserted in the center comes out clean.

FRANCIS M. GIBSON,
CEDAR GROVE ESTATE, VICKSBURG, MS

EGGPLANT PARMESAN

Serve the fried eggplant strips accompanied by the spicy sauce for an irresistible nibble.

Preparation Time: 30-45 minutes, including frying
Serves: 6-8

Facing page: Hot Crab-Cheese Canapes (left) and Eggplant Parmesan (right).

INGREDIENTS

3 medium eggplants, cut into ½-inch strips
2 cups flour
2 cups milk
1 egg
¼ tsp garlic powder
4 tbsps grated Parmesan cheese
Shortening or cooking oil for deep-fat frying

SAUCE

¼ cup horseradish
1 cup mayonnaise

METHOD

Combine the milk and egg in one bowl and the flour and garlic powder in another. Dip the strips of eggplant first in the milk and then in the flour. Heat the oil to 375°F or until a 1-inch cube of bread turns golden in one minute. Fry the eggplant until golden brown and drain on paper towels. To prepare the sauce, combine the horseradish and mayonnaise in a small bowl.

CARL ANDRÉ FLOWERS,
CEDAR GROVE ESTATE, VICKSBURG, MS

HOT CRAB-CHEESE CANAPES

It's difficult to say how many people these canapes will serve, because it's impossible to eat just one!

Preparation Time: 15 minutes
Cooking Time: 2-3 minutes
Yield: 48-72 canapes

INGREDIENTS

1 6oz can crab meat
4oz Old English Sharp Cheddar cheese
1 stick butter or margarine
1 tbsp mayonnaise
1 tsp lemon pepper
1 tsp garlic salt
1 tsp seasoned salt
Dash pepper sauce
Dash Worcestershire sauce
12 English muffins

METHOD

Cut the cheese and butter or margarine into pieces and place in the bowl of a food processor along with the crab meat, mayonnaise and seasonings. Blend until smooth. Split the English muffins and spread with the mixture. Cut each split muffin into 4 or 6 wedges and heat under the broiler until warm. You can also freeze the wedges until needed and broil from frozen.

HELEN MARIE ABRAHAM,
CEDAR GROVE ESTATE, VICKSBURG, MS

BOURBON RIBS

Try these for one of the best barbecues you have ever tasted.

Preparation Time: 20 minutes
Cooking Time: 55 minutes, plus 45 minutes grilling on a barbecue
Serves: 6

INGREDIENTS

4lbs beef or pork ribs

SAUCE

1 medium onion, chopped (approximately ½ cup)
½ cup light molasses
½ cup catsup
2 tsps orange peel, finely shredded
⅓ cup orange juice
2 tbsps cooking oil
1 tbsp vinegar
1 tbsp steak sauce
½ tsp prepared mustard
½ tsp Worcestershire sauce
¼ tsp garlic powder
¼ tsp salt
¼ tsp pepper
¼ tsp hot pepper sauce
⅛ tsp ground cloves
¼ cup bourbon

METHOD

Place the ribs in a large Dutch oven or saucepan and add water to cover. Bring to the boil, then reduce the heat and simmer, covered, for 40-55 minutes or until the ribs are tender. Remove from the heat and drain thoroughly. While the ribs are

Above: Hot 'n' Spicy Red Beans and Rice.

Preparation Time: 15 minutes
Cooking Time: 5½-6½ hours in a crock pot or over a low fire
Serves: 6

INGREDIENTS

*1lb dried red beans
1lb spicy pork sausage
3 medium onions, chopped
1½ tsps salt
1½ tsps pepper
1 tbsp rosemary
1 tbsp thyme
1 tbsp tarragon
1 tbsp oregano*

METHOD

Rinse the beans and soak in water for approximately 30 minutes. Drain, then cook in just enough water to cover for about 30 minutes over a low fire or in a crock pot. Add the remaining ingredients, cover and simmer for 5-6 hours, or until the beans are tender. Stir occasionally during the cooking time, especially at the beginning to break up the sausage meat.

HELEN MARIE ABRAHAM,
CEDAR GROVE ESTATE, VICKSBURG, MS

BELL PEPPER BAKED BEANS

A quick and easy way to enjoy baked beans, Mississippi style!

Preparation Time: 15 minutes
Cooking Time: 25-35 minutes
Serves: 6

INGREDIENTS

*1 16oz can baked beans
1 large bell pepper, cut into small strips
1 small onion, chopped
1 tbsp paprika
1 tbsp prepared mustard
3 tbsps brown sugar
⅛ tsp powdered dried basil
⅛ tsp powdered dried oregano*

cooking, prepare the sauce by combining all of the sauce ingredients in a pan. Bring the mixture to the boil and simmer gently, uncovered, for 15 to 20 minutes.

When the ribs are tender and the sauce is prepared, grill the ribs over slow coals on a barbecue for about 45 minutes. Turn every 15 minutes and baste with the sauce. Extra sauce can be served with the meat.

CARL ANDRÉ FLOWERS,
CEDAR GROVE ESTATE, VICKSBURG, MS

HOT 'N' SPICY RED BEANS AND RICE

These taste-tempting beans should be served over cooked rice. Leftovers are unlikely, but if you have any, they freeze beautifully.

METHOD

Combine all the ingredients in a large baking dish. Bake, uncovered, for 25-35 minutes at 350°F, or until the sauce is thick and the onion and pepper are tender.

CARL ANDRÉ FLOWERS,
CEDAR GROVE ESTATE, VICKSBURG, MS

CRISPY FRIED CATFISH

Preparation Time: 45 minutes
Cooking Time: 10-15 minutes
Serves: 6

INGREDIENTS

6 catfish
½ cup evaporated milk
1 tbsp salt
Dash pepper
1 egg
1 cup flour
½ cup yellow cornmeal
2 tsps paprika
Oil or lard for frying

METHOD

Clean, skin, wash and dry the catfish before cutting them into serving-sized portions. Beat the egg into the milk and stir in the salt and pepper. In a separate bowl, combine the flour, cornmeal and paprika. Dip the cleaned fish in the milk mixture, then roll in the seasoned flour. Heat the oil or lard to 375°F on a fat thermometer, or until a 1-inch cube of bread turns golden after 1 minute, in a heavy-bottomed pan. When the oil is hot enough, add the fish and brown well on both sides. When the fish are well browned, lift them carefully from the pan and drain them on absorbent paper. Serve very hot.

Some cooks prefer to soak the catfish in buttermilk for several hours before frying.

ANN HALL, GREY OAKS,
VICKSBURG, MS

Facing page: Old-Fashioned Coleslaw (left) and Old South Turnip Greens and Pot Liquor (right). Main dish: Crispy Fried Catfish and Hush Puppies.

HUSH PUPPIES

Hush Puppies were originally made out of leftover corn bread batter. Serve them with meat and chicken.

Preparation Time: 20 minutes
Cooking Time: 10 minutes
Yield: approximately 24 Hush Puppies

INGREDIENTS

1 egg, well beaten
⅔ cup milk
1½ cups white cornmeal
½ cup flour, sifted
½ tsp sugar
1 tsp baking powder
½ tsp salt
1 bunch (approximately 1 cup) fresh green onions, finely chopped
Pinch red pepper
Pinch garlic powder
Oil for deep-fat frying

METHOD

Mix together the eggs, milk, cornmeal, flour, sugar, baking powder and salt until well blended and smooth. Add the green onions, red pepper and garlic powder. Shape the dough into small balls. If the dough is too soft, add more cornmeal. Fry the Hush Puppies in deep fat which has been heated to 360°F until they are browned. Drain on absorbent paper.

ANN HALL, GREY OAKS,
VICKSBURG, MS

OLD-FASHIONED COLESLAW

This delicious coleslaw is perfect for an outdoor party or picnic. You can scale down the recipe for smaller groups.

Preparation Time: 30 minutes
Serves: 12

INGREDIENTS

2 medium heads cabbage, finely shredded
2 large carrots, finely shredded

DRESSING

2 cups mayonnaise
1 tsp sugar
½ tsp dried mustard
½ tsp pepper
⅓ cup vinegar or lemon juice
1 tsp salt

METHOD

Toss the cabbage and carrots together to make up the salad. Combine the dressing ingredients and blend well. Pour the dressing over the vegetables and mix well. Chill the coleslaw before serving.

ANN HALL, GREY OAKS,
VICKSBURG, MS

CRAWFISH ETOUFFEE

Preparation Time: 30 minutes
Cooking Time: 35 minutes
Serves: 4-6

INGREDIENTS

6 tbsps salted butter
¼ cup flour
1 large onion, chopped
½ cup chopped green pepper
½ cup chopped celery
1 tbsp garlic, finely minced
30 crawfish tails
½ cup crawfish fat, refrigerated
1 tsp salt
¼ tsp freshly ground black pepper
¼ tsp cayenne
1 tsp fresh lemon juice
⅓ cup thinly sliced green shallot or scallion tops
1 tbsp finely minced fresh parsley
1 cup cold water
2 cups hot water

METHOD

Melt the butter over a low heat in a heavy 5-6 quart kettle. Gradually add the flour, and cook over a low heat until a medium brown roux is formed. Stir in the chopped vegetables. Continue to cook, stirring frequently, until the vegetables are

glazed and tender, about 20 minutes. Add the crawfish tails, crawfish fat, salt, pepper, cayenne, lemon juice, shallot tops and parsley and mix well. Pour in the cold water and bring to the boil. Lower the heat and simmer for 12 minutes, or until the crawfish tails are just tender, stirring frequently. Before serving, stir in up to 2 cups of hot water to provide extra gravy.

The etouffee may be served in patty shells as a first course, or you can serve it over boiled rice as a main dish. Substitute lobster meat for the crawfish if you like.

MARTIN LAFFEY,
DELTA POINT RIVER RESTAURANT,
VICKSBURG, MS

BREASTS OF CHICKEN VICKSBURG

This delicious chicken is sure to be as popular with your guests as it is with the guests at the Magnolia Inn in Vicksburg

Preparation Time: 30 minutes
Cooking Time: 45 minutes
Serves: 6

INGREDIENTS

6 chicken breasts, split and skinned
¼ cup flour
2½ tsps salt
1 tsp paprika
½ cup butter
¼ cup water
2 tsps cornstarch
1½ cups half and half or light cream
¼ cup sherry
1 cup mushrooms, sliced
1 cup Swiss cheese, grated
½ cup fresh parsley, chopped

TO SERVE

6 slices of bread, toasted and with the crusts removed
6 thin slices of cooked ham

METHOD

Coat the chicken pieces with a mixture of the flour, salt and paprika. Melt half of the butter in a heavy skillet with a cover. Lightly brown the chicken in the hot butter, then add the water and simmer the chicken, covered, for 30 minutes, or until tender. Remove the chicken and set aside. Blend ¼ cup of the half and half into cornstarch. Add this to the drippings in the skillet and cook over a low heat, stirring constantly. Gradually add the rest of the half and half and the sherry. Continue cooking and stirring until the sauce is smooth and thickened. Add the grated cheese to the hot sauce and blend until the cheese is melted. Sauté the mushrooms in the remaining butter, drain and add to the sauce. Gently warm the ham slices.

To serve, place the pieces of toast on a large, oblong platter. Top each with a slice of warm ham, then a chicken breast. Cover each serving with the hot sauce. Garnish with chopped parsley and paprika. The serving may also be arranged separately in small individual casserole dishes.

MARTIN LAFFEY,
DELTA POINT RIVER RESTAURANT,
VICKSBURG, MS

ORANGE-GLAZED SOUTHERN HENS

This makes a very special dinner for 2.

Preparation Time: 30-45 minutes
Cooking Time: 1 hour
Serves: 2

INGREDIENTS

1 Cornish hen (1-1½ lbs)
¼ cup butter

Below: Breasts of Chicken Vicksburg.

1 6oz package long-grain and wild rice mix
1 4oz can chopped mushrooms, drained
¼ cup orange peel, cut into julienne strips
3½ tbsps light brown sugar
2¼ tbsps cornstarch
⅔ cup water
¾ cup orange juice
¼ tsp salt
1½ tbsps brandy

METHOD

Rinse the hen and pat dry. Brush with butter and salt and bake at 350°F for 1 hour, brushing occasionally with more butter. Meanwhile, cook the rice according to the package directions. When the rice is cooked, stir in the mushrooms and heat through. Set aside to keep warm while you prepare the sauce.

First, simmer the orange peel in a small amount of water in a covered saucepan for 15 minutes. Drain well and set aside. In another saucepan, combine the brown sugar and cornstarch. Blend in the water and orange juice and cook and stir over a low heat until the sauce is thickened, about 2-3 minutes. Remove from the heat and stir in the orange peel and brandy. Arrange the hen on a serving platter and spoon the sauce on top. Serve with the rice.

CARL ANDRÉ FLOWERS,
CEDAR GROVE ESTATE, VICKSBURG, MS

BAKED TOMATOES STUFFED WITH ENGLISH PEAS

These delicious stuffed tomatoes make a colorful and appetizing start to any special meal.

Preparation Time: 30 minutes
Cooking Time: 20-25 minutes
Serves: 4-6

INGREDIENTS

STUFFING

2 17oz cans small English peas, drained
¼ cup butter or margarine
1 2oz jar chopped pimentos, drained
Salt and pepper to taste

TOMATO SHELLS

4-6 large, firm tomatoes
Salt and pepper to taste

METHOD

To prepare the filling, combine all of the stuffing ingredients in a saucepan. Heat over a moderate fire until the butter melts and the peas are warmed through. Set aside in a warm place while you prepare the tomatoes. Wash the tomatoes and cut off the tops. Scoop out the pulp and set aside to use in other recipes. Sprinkle the insides of the tomatoes with salt and pepper. Fill each shell with the warm peas. Place in a greased baking dish and bake at 300°F for 20-25 minutes, or until the tomato shells are soft.

HELEN MARIE ABRAHAM,
CEDAR GROVE ESTATE, VICKSBURG, MS

PLANTATION RIB-EYE ROAST WITH MUSHROOM GRAVY

You can also serve this roast with Ann's Bernaise Sauce.

Preparation Time: 15 minutes
Cooking Time: 2 hours
Serves: 10-12

INGREDIENTS

8-9lb rib-eye roast
Cracked peppercorns
Garlic salt
Rosemary

MUSHROOM GRAVY

2 tbsps pan drippings from the roast
2 tbsps flour
1 tbsp butter
1 cup fresh mushrooms, sliced
1 cup dry red wine
1 cup beef broth

Facing page: Orange-Glazed Southern Hens and Baked Tomatoes Stuffed with English Peas.

METHOD

Preheat the oven to 500°F. To cook the roast, rub the meat all over with the peppercorns, garlic salt and rosemary. Arrange the roast in a shallow pan and place in the oven. Cook the roast for 5-6 minutes per pound, then turn off the oven, but do not open the door. Leave the roast in the closed oven for a total of two hours. When you open the oven, the roast will be fully cooked and ready to serve.

To prepare the mushroom gravy, make a roux by blending the drippings, butter and flour in a skillet over a moderate heat. Stir in the mushrooms, then gradually add the broth and red wine. Simmer to allow the gravy to thicken and develop more flavor before serving.

ANN HALL, GREY OAKS,
VICKSBURG, MS

ANN'S BERNAISE SAUCE

Serve this special Bernaise sauce with Plantation Rib-Eye Roast.

Preparation Time: 10 minutes
Cooking Time: 10-15 minutes
Yield: approximately 2 cups

INGREDIENTS

6 egg yolks, beaten
2 tbsps tarragon vinegar
4 tbsps half and half or light cream
½ tsp salt
Several dashes cayenne
½ cup butter, melted
4 tsps parsley
1 tsp tarragon leaves
4 tsps chives
½ tsp ground thyme
2 tsps basil leaves
½ tsp minced garlic

METHOD

Combine the egg yolks with the vinegar, half and half, salt and cayenne pepper in the top of a double boiler. Cook over low heat, stirring constantly, until the mixture just begins to thicken. Add the butter, one tablespoon at a time, and stir well after each addition. Blend in the remaining ingredients. This sauce tastes better if prepared a day before it is needed,

but will keep well in the refrigerator for several weeks. If the sauce becomes too thick, a small amount of water may be added to thin it.

ANN HALL, GREY OAKS,
VICKSBURG, MS

OLD SOUTH TURNIP GREENS AND POT LIQUOR

Here is real down home cooking at its best!

Preparation Time: 30 minutes
Cooking Time: 2 hours
Serves: 8

INGREDIENTS

2lbs salt pork
8 cups cold water
1 tsp crushed red pepper
2 tsps salt
½ tsp pepper
6lbs young, tender turnip greens, washed several times

TO SERVE

Sliced hard-boiled eggs
Sliced green onions
Pot liquor

METHOD

In a large pot, combine the salt pork, water, red pepper, salt and pepper. Bring to a boil, then reduce the heat, cover and cook slowly for 1 hour. Add the well washed turnip greens and cook, covered, over a low heat for a further hour, or until the greens and pork are tender. To serve, remove the turnip greens from the pot. Chop them and arrange them in a large serving dish. Place the pork on top and garnish with slices of hard-boiled egg and green onions. Pour the pot liquor over the dish before serving.

ANN HALL, GREY OAKS,
VICKSBURG, MS

HEARTY SPINACH SALAD

This salad is substantial enough to be served as a light luncheon dish.

Above: Old South Turnip Greens and Pot Liquor.

GREEN GODDESS SALAD DRESSING

Serve this dressing with Hearty Spinach Salad. It is also nice to keep this dressing on hand to add a special note to other summer salads.

Preparation Time: 10 minutes
Yield: 2½ cups

INGREDIENTS

1 cup mayonnaise
½ cup sour cream
3 tbsps tarragon vinegar
2 tbsps anchovy paste
1 tsp Worcestershire sauce
½ tsp dry mustard
3 tbsps minced chives
⅓ cup snipped parsley
1 clove garlic, minced
½ tsp salt
½ tsp pepper

METHOD

Combine all ingredients and blend well. The dressing should be refrigerated and will keep well for several days. It tastes best if made the day before serving.

ANN HALL, GREY OAKS,
VICKSBURG, MS

Preparation Time: 15 minutes
Serves: 6

INGREDIENTS

1lb spinach
½lb fresh mushrooms, sliced
3 hard-boiled eggs, sliced
6 slices bacon, cooked and crumbled

METHOD

Wash the spinach thoroughly and tear it into bite-sized pieces. Toss the spinach with the mushrooms, eggs and bacon in a large salad bowl. Pour Green Goddess Salad Dressing over and serve at once.

ANN HALL, GREY OAKS,
VICKSBURG, MS

"ESTELLE" COCKTAIL

INGREDIENTS

1½ jigger crème de banane liqueur
3 jiggers half and half or light cream
1 cup shaved or crushed ice

METHOD

Combine all ingredients in a cocktail shaker. Serve in a champagne goblet, topped with whipped cream and decorated with a sprig of mint and a twist of lime.

CARL ANDRÉ FLOWERS,
CEDAR GROVE ESTATE, VICKSBURG, MS

JEFFERSON DAVIS PIE

Named in honor of one of the heroes of the Confederacy, this pie is sure to please.

Preparation Time: 20 minutes
Cooking Time: 50-60 minutes
Serves: 8

INGREDIENTS

1 tbsp flour
1 tbsp cornmeal
2 cups sugar
4 eggs
¼ cup butter, melted
¼ cup lemon juice
1 tbsp grated lemon rind
¼ cup milk
1 9-inch unbaked pie shell

METHOD

Sift the flour and cornmeal into the sugar. Beat the eggs slightly and add to the sugar mixture, blending well. Add the butter, lemon juice, lemon rind and milk. Pour this filling into the unbaked pie shell. Bake at 350°F for 50-60 minutes or until the filling is set and the center is firm.

MARTIN LAFFEY,
DELTA POINT RIVER RESTAURANT,
VICKSBURG, MS

CHERRIES JUBILEE

This spectacular dessert is really simple to make, and delicious to eat!

Preparation Time: 15 minutes
Cooking Time: 5-10 minutes, plus flaming
Serves: 4-6

INGREDIENTS

1 17oz can pitted fancy Oregon Bing cherries
4 tbsps butter
¼ cup sugar

Jefferson Davis Pie.

Above: Bourbon Pie.

1 tbsp cornstarch
¼ cup brandy

TO SERVE

Vanilla ice cream

METHOD

In a bowl, stir ½ cup of the cherry juice into the cornstarch and set aside. Melt the butter and sugar in a heavy skillet over a low heat. Add the cherries and the rest of the juice to the skillet and stir to coat, then blend in the cornstarch mixture. Cook and stir over low heat until thickened. Place the mixture in a warm chafing dish. When ready to serve, pour the brandy over the cherries and ignite. When the flames die down, serve over vanilla ice cream.

CRAIG R. GIBSON,
CEDAR GROVE ESTATE, VICKSBURG, MS

BOURBON PIE

This pie looks as elegant as it tastes!

Preparation Time: 45 minutes, plus 1-2 hours chilling
Cooking Time: approximately 20 minutes
Serves 8

INGREDIENTS

CHOCOLATE CRUST
1½ cups chocolate wafer crumbs
1 tbsp sugar
4 tbsps unsalted butter or margarine, melted

PIE FILLING

21 large marshmallows
1 cup evaporated milk
1 cup whipping cream
3 tbsps bourbon
½ cup chopped pecans (optional)

TOPPING

1 cup whipping cream
2 tbsps powdered sugar
1½ tsps vanilla extract
2-3oz semi-sweet chocolate, grated

METHOD

First prepare the crust by tossing all ingredients together until the crumbs are moist. Pat the mixture into the bottom and sides of a 9-inch pie pan. Bake in an oven, preheated to 350°F, for 10-12 minutes. Cool, then cover and refrigerate until needed.

To make the filling, combine the marshmallows and the evaporated milk in a heavy 3-quart saucepan or double boiler and cook over medium heat until the marshmallows melt, stirring often. Be careful not to allow the mixture to boil. Cover and refrigerate for approximately 1-2 hours. When the marshmallow mixture is chilled, whip the cream and the bourbon together until stiff peaks form. Fold into the chilled marshmallow mixture along with the pecans, if used. Pour the filling into the prepared crust, smooth the top and chill until set, about 4-5 hours.

Before serving, prepare the topping. With an electric mixer, beat all the topping ingredients together, except for the grated chocolate, until stiff peaks form. Spread over the chilled and set pie. Garnish with the grated chocolate.

HELEN MARIE ABRAHAM,
CEDAR GROVE ESTATE, VICKSBURG, MS

Below: Cherries Jubilee.

LOUISIANA

Ten different flags have flown over the state of Louisiana—the Bayou State—since it was claimed for Spain by the explorer Hernando de Soto in 1541. Louisiana has been under the control of France, Britain, Spain, and the West Florida Republic at various times during its history, and declared itself an independent state in 1861, before joining the Confederacy. The first European colonists in the region came from France, and it was they who named this flat Mississipi delta land Louisiana, after King Louis XIV of France. Louis XV gave Louisiana to King Carlos of Spain in 1763, but several decades later Napoleon Bonaparte forced Spain to return it to France. The territory was eventually sold to the United States for 25 million dollars in 1803.

The landscape over much of Louisiana, with its mild winters and hot, humid summers, is flat, and some of the land is actually below sea level. This is a watery landscape full of swamps and marshes and punctuated by bayous—narrow, sluggish rivers surrounded by wetlands—which are home to many fish, shellfish, and water birds, and much loved by sportsmen.

In spite of its varied past, the main accent in Louisiana is French. New Orleans was the last and greatest of the French territorial capitals in North America. Two main cultures, the Creole and Cajun, developed in southern Louisiana. New Orleans is the home of the Creoles, people of mixed French and Spanish parentage whose offspring often had Negro blood. By contrast, the swamps and bayous upstream are the land of the Cajuns, decendants of the French-speaking Acadians who were expelled from Nova Scotia by the British in 1755.

LOUISIANA

The two groups developed distinctive cuisines, both based on the French tradition. The Creole kitchen is very much in the grand French manner with its delicate blends of herbs, subtle combinations of foods, and separate sauces. The essential ingredients in Creole cooking are said to include an iron pot, preferably well used, brown roux, rich stocks, herbs and spices, and a judicious use of spirits. Cajun cooking incorporates all of these elements, but in a much simpler form. The Cajun dishes are spicier and tend to be made in one pot. In contrast to the elegant metropolitan flavor of Creole cooking, Cajun cuisine is strong country food.

The two traditions have many elements in common. Rice is the staple of both cuisines, and both make extensive use of the abundant Louisiana seafood. Gumbos and stocks are produced in abundance in this land where cooks seem to be born, not made, and there are as many gumbo recipes as there are cooks. Filé powder, made from the dried leaves of sassafras trees, is an important ingredient in gumbos and stews. It imparts a delicate flavor and thickens stocks into a rich gravy. Louisiana cooks transform vegetables such as eggplants and mirlitons, a type of tropical squash with firm, crisp white flesh, into gourmet dishes when they fill them with delicious seafood stuffings. The crawfish, always pronounced as it's spelled, is an important basis for many Creole and Cajun masterpieces, ranging from the elegant crawfish bisque with stuffed crawfish heads to the more rustic crawfish boil. The careful preparation of stocks and sauces is all-important. Of these, the many variations of the roux are most often used. The Creole roux, like their French counterparts, are based on a mixture of flour and butter, which is gently cooked to achieve the required color. Cajun roux are made from oil and flour, and are much darker and more robust.

The recipes in this collection come from Lafitte's Landing in Donaldson, Louisiana. Donaldson is located in Cajun country on the banks of the Mississippi, north of New Orleans, but south of Baton Rouge, the state capital. Lafitte's Landing is well placed to provide samples of the two great traditions, and the recipes range from the elaborate to the simple. What they all have in common is the original use of local ingredients and invigorating seasonings which makes Louisiana cooking among the most innovative in America.

Facing page: Crawfish Boil.

RIVER ROAD SEAFOOD GUMBO

Above: River Road Seafood Gumbo.

Preparation Time: 45 minutes
Cooking Time: 50 minutes
Serves: 10

INGREDIENTS

*2lbs 35 count shrimp, peeled and deveined (reserve
shells to make shellfish stock)*
1½ cups oil
2 cups flour
2 cups chopped onions

1 cup chopped celery
¾ cup chopped bell pepper
¼ cup chopped garlic
*1lb andouille or other high quality
smoked sausage, diced*
1lb claw crab meat
1 gallon shellfish stock
2 cups scallions, sliced
2 dozen oysters, shelled
Liquor from the oysters
¼ cup parsley, chopped
¼ tbsp filé powder (optional) or tapioca flour
Salt and cayenne pepper to taste

METHOD

Add the oil to a heavy-bottomed stock pot and heat over medium heat. When the oil is hot, add the flour. Using a wire whisk, stir constantly until a light brown roux is achieved, being careful not to let the roux scorch. Add the onions. Sauté for approximately 2 minutes then add the celery, bell pepper, garlic and the white part of the scallions. Cook for 2 minutes, stirring constantly. Add the smoked sausage and blend well into the roux mixture. Stir in the crab meat and 1lb of the shrimp. Blend well into the roux until the shrimp begin to turn pink. Add the shellfish stock, 1 ladle at a time, blending after each addition until it is well incorporated. Continue adding stock until the gumbo achieves a soup-like texture. Simmer the gumbo for 35 minutes, adding remaining stock to retain the volume. Add half of the scallion tops, the oyster liquor, remaining shrimp and parsley. Cook for 5 minutes then add the oysters, remaining scallions and filé powder or tapioca flour. Remove the gumbo from the heat and allow to stand for 15 minutes. Season to taste with salt and cayenne pepper.

Serve this classic gumbo in a large bowl over rice.

JOHN D. FOLSE, LAFITTE'S LANDING,
P.O. BOX 1128, DONALDSONVILLE, LA

CRAWFISH BOIL

One of the greatest summer social events in South Louisiana is the Crawfish Boil. Everyone pitches in to help prepare the enormous pot of crawfish. And everyone eats more than they ever believed possible. Needless to say, a wonderful time is had by all.

Preparation Time: 1 hour
Cooking Time: 45 minutes
Serves: 25

INGREDIENTS

5lbs salt
1lb cayenne pepper
2lb medium onions, quartered
6 heads garlic, split in half to expose the cloves
12 lemons, cut in half
1 quart cooking oil
9oz pickling spices
30 quarts water
5lbs medium new potatoes, diced
25 ears corn, shucked and cut into thick slices
80lbs live crawfish

METHOD

Place all ingredients except for the potatoes, corn and crawfish in a 60 quart stock pot and bring to a boil over a medium-high heat. Boil for 20 minutes, adding extra water to retain the volume. Meanwhile, rinse the crawfish in a large wash tub to remove all foreign debris and mud. Discard any dead crawfish.

Add the potatoes and corn to the pot and boil for approximately 5 minutes before adding the crawfish. Return to the boil and boil for 7 minutes. Remove from the heat and leave to stand for a further 15 minutes. Remove the crawfish and vegetables from the brine before serving.

JOHN D. FOLSE, LAFITTE'S LANDING,
P.O. BOX 1128, DONALDSONVILLE, LA

OYSTERS JEAN LAFITTE

You can really put your culinary skills to the test with this fine example of the French influence on Louisiana Cajun cuisine.

Preparation Time: 1 hour
Cooking Time: 20 minutes
Serves: 4

INGREDIENTS

OYSTERS
12 select oysters
1 cup milk
1 small egg
3 tsps salt
½ tsp black pepper
½ tsp white pepper
½ tsp cayenne pepper
½ tsp granulated garlic
1 cup cornmeal
Oil for deep fat frying

CROUTONS
12 slices French bread
¼ cup butter, melted
1 tsp granulated garlic

BROWN MEUNIÈRE SAUCE

¼ cup prepared Demi-Glace (see recipe)
¼ cup dry white wine
loz lemon juice
½ lb cold, unsalted butter
Salt and cayenne pepper to taste

METHOD

Begin by preparing the oysters. Beat the egg and combine with the milk and half of each of the seasonings. Soak the oysters in the milk. Meanwhile, combine the rest of the seasonings with the cornmeal. Take the oysters from the milk, allowing excess liquid to drain off, and dredge them in the seasoned cornmeal. Fry in deep fat, heated to 375°F, for 5-7 minutes depending on size or until golden brown. Drain on absorbent paper. Keep warm while you prepare the rest of the dish.

To prepare the croutons, brush the bread with melted butter. Sprinkle on the granulated garlic and toast in a 400°F oven until light brown. Keep warm while you make the meunière sauce.

In a saucepan, combine the previously prepared demi-glace, wine and lemon juice. Reduce over a medium-high heat to approximately 4 ounces in volume. Cut the butter into ½-inch pieces. Add to the saucepan 3 pieces at a time, stirring constantly with a wire whisk. When all the butter has been incorporated, remove the sauce from the heat. Season to taste with salt and cayenne pepper.

While the sauce is warm, assemble the dish. Arrange the croutons on a plate and top with the fried oysters. Cover the oysters with some of the brown meunière sauce and serve immediately. Extra sauce can be served separately using an empty oyster shell as a dish.

JOHN D. FOLSE, LAFITTE'S LANDING,
P.O. BOX 1128, DONALDSONVILLE, LA

SHRIMP VIALA

Wonderful Louisiana seafood is combined in this classic dish.

Preparation Time: 1 hour
Marinading Time: 1 hour
Cooking Time: 25 minutes
Serves: 4 as a main course, 8 as a first course

Oysters Jean Lafitte.

INGREDIENTS

2 dozen extra large shrimp, with heads on

MARINADE

½lb butter, melted
½ cup lemon juice
½ cup sherry
6 cloves garlic, chopped
3 bay leaves, crushed
2 tsps cracked black peppercorns
Salt and cayenne pepper to taste

WHITE SAUCE

½ cup milk
1 bay leaf
1 slice onion
3 peppercorns
1 tbsp butter
1 tbsp flour
Salt and pepper to taste

STUFFING

¼ cup butter
¼ cup onions, diced
¼ cup celery, diced
¼ cup pimentos
2 cloves garlic
¼ cup scallions, chopped
½ tsp Dijon mustard
½ tsp Pernod
1 tbsp sherry
¾lb crab meat

METHOD

Preheat the oven to 350°F. Place the shrimp right-side-up on a cutting board. Using a sharp knife, cut through the shell lengthwise from the top of the tail, making sure not to separate the head from the tail. Remove the vein. Combine all the marinade ingredients in a baking pan. Place the shrimp tail down in the marinade and leave for approximately 1 hour.

Meanwhile, make the white sauce. Combine the milk, bay leaf, onion slice and peppercorns in a saucepan and bring to the boil. Remove from the heat and leave to stand for 15 minutes. Melt the butter and stir in the flour to make a smooth paste. Cook briefly over a moderate heat, stirring constantly. Strain the milk and gradually add to the flour, stirring constantly. Bring to the boil and simmer until the sauce is thick enough to coat the back of a spoon. Set the white sauce aside to add to the stuffing.

To prepare the stuffing, combine the butter, onions, celery, garlic and scallions in a sauté pan. Sauté for approximately 5 minutes, until limp but not brown. Remove from the heat and turn into a mixing bowl. Add the remaining stuffing ingredients and the white sauce. Season to taste with salt and cayenne pepper.

Use this stuffing to stuff the shrimp tails. Bake the stuffed shrimp for 15-20 minutes. Serve over seasoned rice for a main course, or with heated marinade for a first course.

JOHN D. FOLSE, LAFITTE'S LANDING,
P.O. BOX 1128, DONALDSONVILLE, LA

OYSTERS ROCKEFELLER

This makes a delicious and elegant first course.

Preparation Time: 30 minutes
Cooking Time: 50 minutes
Serves: 8

INGREDIENTS

¼lb butter
1 cup chopped onions
1 cup chopped celery
½ cup chopped parsley
1 cup chopped scallions
4 cloves garlic, chopped
2 10oz packages frozen spinach, cooked
1 cup lettuce, chopped
2oz anchovies, mashed
¼ cup oyster liquor
Dash Tabasco sauce
Dash Worcestershire sauce
¼ cup anise flavored liqueur
2 tbsps cream
¼ cup seasoned Italian bread crumbs
Salt and cayenne pepper to taste
2 dozen oysters on the half shell

METHOD

Preheat the oven to 375°F. First prepare the Rockefeller sauce. In a heavy-bottomed sauté pan, melt the butter over a medium heat. Add the onions, celery, parsley, scallions and garlic and

Facing page: Shrimp Viala.

Facing page: Softshell Crawfish Jean David with Sauce Hollandaise. Above: Oysters Rockefeller.

sauté until transparent, about 5 minutes. Add the spinach and lettuce and cook for 20 minutes, stirring with a metal spoon until all the vegetables are well mixed. Add the anchovies and the oyster liquor and cook for 3 minutes. Blend the mixture in a food processor until smooth, then return to the pan. Stir in the Tabasco sauce, Worcestershire sauce, anise liqueur and cream. Simmer for 2 minutes then add the bread crumbs. The mixture will be thick. Season to taste with salt and cayenne pepper.

Place the oysters on their shells in the oven for approximately 10 minutes. Drain off the excess liquor and top with a large spoonful of the Rockefeller sauce. Return to the oven and bake for 15-20 minutes, or until bubbly.

JOHN D. FOLSE, LAFITTE'S LANDING,
P.O. BOX 1128, DONALDSONVILLE, LA

SOFTSHELL CRAWFISH JEAN DAVID WITH SAUCE HOLLANDAISE

Two types of crawfish are combined in this delicious concoction.

Preparation Time: 40 minutes
Cooking Time: 20 minutes
Serves: 2 as a main course, or 4 as an appetizer

INGREDIENTS

6 tbsps butter
2 cloves garlic, chopped
1 tsp fresh parsley
Juice of ½ lemon

½lb crawfish tails
½oz white wine
1 cup milk
1 egg, beaten
16 Louisiana softshell crawfish
2 cups yellow cornmeal, seasoned to taste
Oil for deep frying

HOLLANDAISE SAUCE

4oz unsalted butter
1 tbsp white vinegar
1 tbsp water
1 tbsp white wine
2 egg yolks
Few drops lemon juice
Salt and cayenne pepper to taste

METHOD

In a sauté pan, melt the butter and add the garlic and parsley. Sauté over medium heat until the butter begins to brown, but be careful not to let it burn. Add the lemon juice and the crawfish tails. Stir briskly until the crawfish are heated through, then reduce the heat to low before adding the white wine. Set aside and keep warm.

In a separate bowl, beat together the egg and milk. Soak the softshell crawfish in this mixture, then remove, drain and roll in the seasoned cornmeal. Fry in deep fat which has been heated to 375°F, until golden brown. Drain on absorbent paper towels.

To prepare the Hollandaise sauce, melt the butter in a small saucepan over medium heat. Set aside and allow to cool slightly. In a separate pan, combine the vinegar, half of the water, the wine and a pinch of salt and pepper. Cook over a medium heat until reduced by half. Stir in the remaining water and allow to cool slightly. Whisk this mixture with the egg yolks in the top of a double boiler until the yolks are the consistency of thick cream. Remove from the heat and slowly pour in the melted butter, whisking continuously. If the sauce is too thick, add a few drops of water. Adjust the seasoning and add the lemon juice.

To serve, top the fried softshell crawfish with the sautéed crawfish and approximately half of the Hollandaise sauce. Reserve the rest of the sauce for another use.

JOHN D. FOLSE, LAFITTE'S LANDING,
P.O. BOX 1128, DONALDSONVILLE, LA

Facing page: Jambalaya.

JAMBALAYA

This classic Louisiana dish is perfect for a large party.

Preparation Time: 30 minutes
Cooking Time: 2 hours
Serves: 10

INGREDIENTS

1lb pork, cut into half inch cubes
1lb boneless chicken meat
4 cups water
1 bell pepper, chopped
1lb onions, chopped
1lb smoked sausage, diced
1 can cream of mushroom soup
1 bunch scallions, chopped
¼ cup parsley, chopped
1lb Uncle Ben's rice
10 drops Worcestershire sauce
1 tbsp garlic powder
Salt and pepper to taste

METHOD

Season the pork with salt, pepper and the garlic powder a few hours before you plan to cook. Pour ½ cup of the water into a 6 quart pot and add the seasoned pork. Cook over medium heat for 30 minutes. Add the chicken and cook for a further 10 minutes. Stir in the onions and bell pepper and continue cooking for 15 minutes, stirring often to avoid sticking. Mix in the smoked sausage and simmer for an additional 10 minutes. Next add the cream of mushroom soup, the rest of the water, the scallions, parsley and rice. Bring to a boil and season to taste. Cover and cook over a low heat for 30 minutes, stirring once after 15 minutes.

JOHN D. FOLSE, LAFITTE'S LANDING,
P.O. BOX 1128, DONALDSONVILLE, LA

STUFFED LEG OF RABBIT À LA CHASSEUR

The crab meat dressing makes an unusual foil for succulent roasted rabbit.

Preparation Time: 40 minutes
Cooking Time: 20 minutes

LOUISIANA

Serves: 6

INGREDIENTS

*4 rabbit haunches (back leg and thigh with the thigh
bone removed)*
2 rashers bacon
2 tbsps butter
1½ cups red wine
½ cup prepared game stock
Salt, cayenne and black pepper to taste

HUNTER SAUCE

3oz butter
1 cup diced mushrooms
(wild Louisiana mushrooms are best)
1 cup scallions, chopped
3 cloves garlic, minced
1 cup ripe tomatoes, chopped
½ cup red wine
¼ cup brandy
1 pint prepared demi-glace made from game stock
¼ cup parsley, chopped
Salt and cayenne pepper to taste

CRAB MEAT DRESSING

¼ cup onions, minced
1 scallion, chopped
1 clove garlic, minced
2 mushrooms, chopped
2 tbsps dry white wine
½lb lump crab meat
2 slices white bread, chopped
1 tsp Pernod
Salt and cayenne pepper to taste

GARNISH

Carrots
Mushrooms
Watercress or parsley

METHOD

Begin by preparing the dressing. In a small sauté pan, sauté
the onions until translucent, over a medium heat. Add the
scallion, garlic and mushrooms and sauté for a further minute.
Deglaze with the white wine and remove from the heat. Add

Shrimp-Stuffed Mirlitons (left), Pattypan Squash with
Black-Eyed and Green Peas (top right), Baked Yams
(center), and Stuffed Leg of Rabbit à la Chasseur
(bottom left and right).

the crab meat and bread and mix well, being careful not to break up the crab meat. Season with Pernod, salt and pepper.

Use this dressing to stuff the deboned rabbit thighs. Secure the ends with toothpicks. Season the rabbit with salt, cayenne and black pepper. Rub each haunch with ½ tablespoon butter and top with ½ of a bacon rasher. Arrange in a cast iron skillet and roast in an oven which has been preheated to 400°F, for 10-15 minutes.

Meanwhile, prepare the Hunter Sauce. In a heavy-bottomed sauté pan, melt the butter over a medium high heat. Sauté the mushrooms, scallions, garlic and tomatoes for 5 minutes. Add the red wine and brandy. Simmer and reduce by three quarters. Add the demi-glace and parsley. Season with salt and cayenne pepper to taste. Simmer over a low heat for 5 minutes, stirring occasionally. Measure 1 cup of the sauce to use now and reserve the rest to serve with other meat dishes.

When the rabbit haunches have roasted, remove them from the skillet. Deglaze the pan over a medium-high heat with the red wine and game stock, scraping free any particles which cling to the bottom of the pan. Add the Hunter Sauce and reduce by simmering until 1 cup of sauce remains.

To serve, divide the sauce between 4 plates. Sever the legs from the thighs and place one leg on each plate. Slice the thighs into 2 or 3 medallions to expose the dressing and arrange in a semi-circle around each leg. Garnish with carrots, mushrooms and watercress or parsley.

JOHN D. FOLSE, LAFITTE'S LANDING,
P.O. BOX 1128, DONALDSONVILLE, LA

PATTYPAN SQUASH WITH BLACK-EYED AND GREEN PEAS

The combination of two types of peas makes an unusual and delicious filling for pretty, scalloped pattypan squash.

Preparation Time: 45 minutes
Cooking Time: 2 hours
Serves: 6

INGREDIENTS

6 pattypan squash
½ lb green peas
¼ tsp lemon juice
Pinch sugar

2 tsps butter
½ lb black-eyed peas (if dried, rinse and soak overnight)
1½ quarts water
1 ham bone
½ cup onions, coarsely chopped
2 cloves garlic, minced
1 bay leaf
½ lb smoked sausage, ham hocks or andouille
¼ cup scallions, chopped
⅛ cup parsley, chopped

METHOD

First prepare the squash by cutting off the tops and carefully scooping out the flesh to leave a firm shell. Reserve the flesh for another use. Boil the shells in lightly-salted water until tender. Drain and set aside.

Cook the green peas in a covered pot in a small amount of water with the lemon juice and sugar. When the peas are tender, drain and stir in the butter. Set aside.

Place the black-eyed peas, water, ham bone, onions, garlic, bay leaf, scallions, parsley, smoked meat and salt and pepper in a heavy saucepan. Bring to the boil over a medium-high heat, then reduce the heat and simmer for 2 hours or until the black-eyed peas are tender, adding more water if needed. Remove the ham bone and bay leaf.

To assemble, fill the squash shells with half green peas and half black-eyed peas.

JOHN D. FOLSE, LAFITTE'S LANDING,
P.O. BOX 1128, DONALDSONVILLE, LA

BAKED YAMS

The special additions make these yams really tasty.

Preparation Time: 15 minutes
Cooking Time: 50 minutes
Serves: 4

INGREDIENTS

6 yams
2 tbsps butter
3 tsps brown sugar
2 tsps Bourbon whiskey
¼ cup cream, warmed
½ tsp salt
Pinch nutmeg

¼ cup raisins
¼ cup toasted pecans

METHOD

Scrub the yams and bake at 400°F for approximately 50 minutes, or until soft. While still hot, scoop out the pulp and mash well. Add the remaining ingredients, except for the pecans and raisins, and whip until fluffy. Fold in the raisins and pecans.

JOHN D. FOLSE, LAFITTE'S LANDING,
P.O. BOX 1128, DONALDSONVILLE. LA

SHRIMP-STUFFED MIRLITONS

Preparation Time: 30 minutes
Cooking Time: 45 minutes
Serves: 8

INGREDIENTS

4 mirlitons
2 tbsps vegetable oil
1 cup onions, chopped
½ cup celery, chopped
2 cloves garlic, chopped
1 cup fresh shrimp, chopped
1 cup seasoned Italian bread crumbs
2 eggs, beaten
¼ cup fresh parsley, chopped
Salt and pepper to taste

METHOD

Slice the mirlitons lengthwise and place in a pot. Add water to cover and boil until tender, then strain and cool. Scoop out the flesh and remove the seeds to leave a hollow shell. Drain the flesh in a colander, then chop finely.

Heat the vegetable oil in a sauté pan and add the onions, garlic and celery. Cook for 5 minutes, then add the shrimp and cook for a further 10 minutes. Add the chopped mirliton flesh and simmer for 15 minutes. Mix in half of the bread crumbs along with the parsley, salt and pepper. Add the eggs and blend well. Cook for approximately 10 minutes.

Use this mixture to fill the mirliton shells. Sprinkle with the remaining bread crumbs and brown in a 350°F oven for approximately 5-10 minutes.

If mirlitons are not available, you can make a similar dish by substituting summer squash.

JOHN D. FOLSE, LAFITTE'S LANDING,
P.O. BOX 1128, DONALDSONVILLE, LA

STUFFED EGGPLANT WITH SHRIMP

Preparation Time: 45 minutes
Cooking Time: 1 hour
Serves: 8

INGREDIENTS

4 medium eggplants
2 tbsps shortening
1 cup chopped onions
1 cup chopped bell pepper
½ cup chopped celery
2 cloves garlic, chopped
½ cup chopped scallions
1lb ground beef
1lb fresh shrimp, chopped
3½ cups seasoned Italian bread crumbs
2 eggs, beaten
Salt and pepper to taste

METHOD

Slice the eggplants lengthwise and place in a pot of lightly salted water. Bring to a rolling boil and cook until tender. Drain, cool and scoop out the flesh, being careful not to tear the shell. Drain the excess water from the flesh and chop finely.

Melt the shortening in a sauté pan over a medium high heat. Sauté the onions, scallions, bell pepper, garlic and celery for approximately five minutes, stirring occasionally. Add the ground beef and blend well into the vegetable mixture. Continue cooking for approximately 20 minutes or until brown. Finally, add the shrimp and chopped eggplant flesh. Cook for about 30 minutes, stirring occasionally to keep from sticking. Add 2½ cups of the seasoned bread crumbs and the beaten eggs and mix well. Season to taste with salt and cayenne pepper. Use this mixture to stuff the eggplant shells. Top with the remaining bread crumbs. Bake at 350°F for 5-10 minutes, or until brown.

The shrimp add a Louisiana flavor to these stuffed

eggplants. You can also serve the filling in a casserole if you don't wish to stuff the eggplant shells.

JOHN D. FOLSE, LAFITTE'S LANDING,
P.O. BOX 1128, DONALDSONVILLE, LA

FROG LEGS

Preparation Time: 15 minutes
Cooking Time: 15 minutes
Serves: 4

INGREDIENTS

½ cup butter
4 tbsps olive oil
6 cloves garlic, minced
1 tbsp cracked black peppercorns
¼ cup scallions, chopped
8 frog legs, approximately 4 inches long
1oz white wine
1 tbsp chopped pimentoes
¼ cup parsley, chopped
½ tsp cayenne pepper
1 tsp salt

GARNISH

4 lemon slices
4 sprigs parsley

METHOD

Melt the butter in a heavy-bottomed sauté pan over a medium-high heat. Add the olive oil, garlic, peppercorns and scallions. Sauté for 1 minute, stirring constantly to prevent the garlic from browning. Add the frog legs and continue to stir and cook until they are opaque in appearance and tender to the touch, approximately 3 minutes. Deglaze with the white wine, then add the pimentoes, parsley, salt and cayenne pepper. Serve the frog legs with the sauce from the pan, garnished with lemon slices and parsley sprigs.

These delicious frog legs are also good served with a Bordelaise sauce.

JOHN D. FOLSE, LAFITTE'S LANDING,
P.O. BOX 1128, DONALDSONVILLE, LA

Frog Legs.

CAJUN STUFFED FILET MIGNON

Seafood and beef are combined in this recipe to make a very elegant dinner for two.

Preparation Time: 40 minutes
Cooking Time: 30 minutes
Serves: 2

INGREDIENTS

2 9oz filet mignons
¼ cup melted butter

1 tbsp crushed thyme
1 tbsp tarragon
1 tbsp sweet basil
1 tbsp rosemary
Salt and cayenne pepper to taste
¾ cup dry red wine

WHITE SAUCE

½ cup milk
1 bay leaf
1 slice onion
3 peppercorns
1 tbsp butter
1 tbsp flour
Salt and pepper to taste

CAJUN CRAB MEAT STUFFING

¾ lb white crab meat
¼ cup diced onions
¼ cup diced celery
¼ cup pimentos
2 cloves garlic, chopped
¼ cup scallions, chopped
½ tsp Dijon mustard
½ tsp Pernod
1 tbsp sherry
1 tbsp fresh parsley, chopped
Salt and cayenne pepper to taste

Facing page: Stuffed Eggplant with Shrimp. Below: Cajun Stuffed Filet Mignon.

METHOD

Trim the excess fat and cut a ¾-inch pocket in the center of each filet. Place the meat in a roasting pan and add the butter and herbs, making sure the herbs are well distributed over each filet. Season with salt and cayenne pepper.

Next prepare the white sauce. Combine the milk, bay leaf, onion slice and peppercorns in a saucepan and bring to the boil. Remove from the heat and leave to stand for 15 minutes. In a separate pan, melt the butter and stir in the flour to make a smooth paste. Cook briefly over a moderate heat, stirring constantly. Strain the milk and gradually add to the flour, stirring constantly. Bring to the boil and simmer until the sauce is thick enough to coat the back of a spoon. Set aside to add to the stuffing.

To prepare the stuffing, combine all of the ingredients and stir in the prepared white sauce. Stuff the pockets in the meat

with this mixture. Roast at 475°F for approximately 15 minutes. Deglaze the roasting pan with ¾ cup of red wine, then reduce the volume by half. Serve as a sauce over the filets.

JOHN D. FOLSE, LAFITTE'S LANDING,
P.O. BOX 1128, DONALDSONVILLE, LA

BROWN ROUX

INGREDIENTS

2oz butter
½ cup flour
1 quart brown stock

METHOD

Heat the butter until it sizzles and stir in the flour to make a smooth paste. Continue to cook over medium heat, stirring constantly until the paste is a nutty brown color. Gradually stir in 1 quart of brown stock.

BLONDE ROUX

INGREDIENTS

2oz butter
½ cup flour
1 quart milk

METHOD

Heat the butter until it sizzles and stir in the flour to make a smooth paste. Continue to cook over a medium heat, stirring constantly until the paste is a light brown color. Gradually add the milk to make a sauce.

JOHN D. FOLSE, LAFITTE'S LANDING,
P.O. BOX 1128, DONALDSONVILLE, LA

BEIGNETS

A night on the town in New Orleans is not complete without stopping for chicory coffee and fresh hot beignets.

Preparation Time: 1 hour
Cooking Time: 15 minutes
Yield: 20 beignets

INGREDIENTS

½ cup milk, warmed to blood temperature
2 tsps dried yeast or ⅓oz fresh yeast
1 egg, beaten
⅛ cup sugar
½ tsp salt
1¾ cups bread flour
⅛ cup butter, softened
Oil for deep fat frying
Confectioners' sugar

METHOD

Dissolve the yeast in the warm milk, then add the sugar, salt and beaten egg. Gradually add half of the flour, stirring until well blended, then mix in the softened butter. Gradually add the rest of the flour until the dough is very stiff and can only be mixed with your hands.

Place the dough in a warm bowl and cover with a towel. Leave it to rise in a warm place for approximately 1 hour, or until it has doubled in bulk. Knead gently on a floured surface, then roll out to a ¼-inch thickness. Cut the dough into rectangles approximately 2½ x 3½ inches and place on a lightly floured pan. Cover with a towel and leave to rise for approximately 35 minutes. Deep fry in oil which has been heated to 360°F, turning once when the bottom side has browned. Drain on paper towels, then dust generously with confectioners' sugar.

JOHN D. FOLSE, LAFITTE'S LANDING,
P.O. BOX 1128, DONALDSONVILLE, LA

FLOATING ISLES

A spectacular and delicious dessert.

Preparation Time: 30 minutes
Cooking Time: 20 minutes
Serves: 6-8

INGREDIENTS

8 eggs, separated
6 cups milk or heavy cream
1½ cups sugar

Facing page: Beignets.

2 tsps cornstarch
3 tbsps vanilla
Pinch cinnamon
Pinch nutmeg

METHOD

First prepare a custard by combining the egg yolks, 1 cup of the sugar, the cornstarch and flavorings. Blend well with a whisk. Heat the milk over a medium heat to scald, but do not boil. Stir approximately 1 cup of the hot milk into the egg mixture to stabilize it. Add the the stabilized egg mixture to the rest of the hot milk and continue cooking over a low heat, stirring constantly until the custard is slightly thickened. When the custard is thick, pour it into a heavy bowl and allow to cool.

Meanwhile, prepare the meringue. In a mixing bowl, beat the egg whites until peaks form. Add the remaining ½ cup of sugar very gradually to form a stiff meringue. Poach the meringue by dropping it by large spoonfuls into hot water and simmering for 2 minutes on each side over a low heat. Remove and drain.

When the custard in cooled, arrange the meringue islands on top.

JOHN D. FOLSE, LAFITTE'S LANDING,
P.O. BOX 1128, DONALDSONVILLE, LA

PRALINE CREPES

If you follow the recipe carefully, you will produce a spectacular and delicious finish to a special meal.

Preparation Time: 2 hours
Cooking Time: 20 minutes
Serves: 6

INGREDIENTS

CREPES
½ cup flour
1½ tsps sugar
Pinch salt
2 eggs
1½ tsps vanilla extract
1 tbsp brandy or cognac
1 tbsp melted butter
¾ cup milk
Butter for frying

PRALINE CREAM FILLING
¼ cup sugar
3 egg yolks
⅛ cup flour
Pinch salt
1 cup milk
½ oz praline-flavored liqueur
¼ cup ground roasted pecans
1½ tsps vanilla extract
1 tbsp unsalted butter, softened

MERINGUE
2 egg whites
⅛ cup sugar

PRALINE SABAYON
3 egg yolks
½ cup sugar
½ cup dry white wine
⅛ cup praline liqueur

TO SERVE
½ cup sliced strawberries
¼ cup toasted pecan halves
Additional strawberries (optional)
Mint leaves (optional)

METHOD

Begin by preparing the crepes. In a large mixing bowl, combine the flour, salt and sugar. Beat in the eggs, one at a time. Add the vanilla, cognac and melted butter. Blend well, then add the milk in a steady stream, whisking constantly. The batter should be the consistency of heavy whipping cream. Heat an 8-inch crepe pan over a medium-high heat. Swirl butter in the pan to coat well. Pour approximately 2 tablespoons of batter into the hot pan and tilt the pan in a circular motion to spread the batter evenly. Cook until the crepe begins to brown along the outer edges and loosens easily with a thin spatula. Turn the crepe, using your fingers, and cook on the other side for 30 seconds. Stack cooked crepes on a heated plate and keep warm.

Next prepare the praline cream filling. In a large mixing bowl, whisk together the sugar and egg yolks until well blended. Gradually add the flour, praline liqueur, vanilla and ground pecans. Season with a pinch of salt. Heat the milk to scalding in a heavy-bottomed saucepan over a medium-high heat. Whisking constantly, pour hot milk into the egg mixture. Return the mixture to the saucepan, beating constantly. Cook over a medium-high heat until the mixture comes to a boil. Boil for 1 minute, then remove from the heat.

Above: Praline Crepes.

Allow to cool slightly, stirring occasionally to prevent a skin from forming. Blend in the softened unsalted butter. Set aside.

Prepare the meringue by beating the egg whites with a wire whisk until soft peaks form. Beat in the sugar, one tablespoon at a time, and continue to beat until the mixture is stiff but not dry.

Lay prepared crepes out flat on a board and place spoonfuls of the praline cream filling in the center of each. Arrange sliced strawberries on top of the filling. Roll up each crepe and place in a baking pan. Pipe the meringue from a pastry bag over the crepes and bake at 400°F for 2-5 minutes or until the meringue is lightly browned.

About 20 minutes before serving, prepare the sabayon. In a heavy-bottomed saucepan, whisk together the egg yolks and sugar until the mixture is thick and creamy, approximately 10 minutes. Place the saucepan over a double boiler containing 3 inches of water. Bring the water to a simmer over a medium-high heat. Slowly add the white wine and praline liqueur while whisking constantly. Continue to whisk until the mixture triples in volume. Remove the saucepan from the water bath and continue to whisk for a further two minutes. The sabayon must be used immediately or it will separate.

Pour warm sabayon onto the center of 6 dinner plates, coating them evenly. Place 2 crepes on the center of each plate and garnish with toasted pecans. Additional strawberries or mint leaves may also be used as a garnish if desired.

JOHN D. FOLSE, LAFFITTE'S LANDING,
P.O. BOX 1128, DONALDSONVILLE, LA

ARKANSAS

Most, people, when they think of Arkansas, think of the Ozark Mountains, rugged hills surrounded by prairies, covered by rich forests, and underlain by natural caves and deep, cool springs. Most early pioneers who traveled west bypassed the Ozarks because of their rocky landscape and poor soil. The Osage indians were native to the area, but they were joined in the early nineteenth century by hardworking settlers from Kentucky, Illinois, and Tennessee, who were used to the rigors of hardscrabble farming. The past survives in the Ozarks as it does nowhere else in the United States. Here women still get together for quilting bees and men swap stories over a game of checkers at the general store. The years of isolation in the rugged mountains have helped to preserve the speech patterns of Elizabethan England brought over with the early settlers. The Ozark accent is unique in the English speaking world.

Although the image of the mountain folk dominates most people's thinking about Arkansas, the Ozarks cover only a quarter of the state. The mighty Mississippi River forms the eastern border of Arkansas. The flat, fertile farmland in the surrounding delta plains is reminiscent of the vast cotton fields of the neighboring state of Mississippi. The swamps and pine forests of the southern part of the state resemble those of Louisiana. Cattle ranches and oil rigs dominate the southwestern part of Arkansas and the navigable Arkansas River, which drains into the Mississippi, has made the capital, Little Rock, a bustling inland port.

Cooking in Arkansas draws heavily on Southern traditions and ingredients, which particular emphasis on real "down-home" flavors. Special favorites include suppers of fried pork chops in a light brown, creamy gravy enriched with tasty bites of sausage meat. Or the sausage meat might be saved to make "dressing," a sustaining and delicious combination of fried sausage meat with cooked rice, stirred and cooked until the meat is done and the mixture is sticky. As elsewhere on the Mississippi, catfish, coated in cornmeal and crisp-fried, is popular. And cornmeal is also used to crisp-fry that most Southern of vegetables, okra.

Okra, the fruit of the *Hibiscus esculentus*, is a native of tropical Africa. Its popular names, okra and gumbo, come from the East African Twi and Umbundu languages. The plant crossed the Atlantic with the slaves and found a new home in the kitchens of the Southern states. Okra is an essential ingredient in Louisiana gumbos, but it is also popular when coated in cornmeal and fried in hot oil to a golden brown. These crisp morsels are delicious as a snack on their own, or when served to accompany meat dishes.

For dessert, that classic American favorite, strawberry shortcake, may well be on a summer menu. Recipes for strawberry shortcake date back to the mid-1600s, when the early settlers were introduced by the Indians to this "wonder of fruits growing naturally in these parts." In Arkansas, the old-fashioned combination of crisp, buttery shortcake, split in half, soaked in strawberry juice, and smothered in whipped cream and fresh strawberries, is still popular with natives and visitors alike.

The recipes in this collection were gathered in Little Rock and chosen to emphasize the traditions of the state. Some of the recipes have come from Liza, the cook at the Governor's Mansion for over thirty years. What she doesn't know about good Arkansas home cooking is probably not work remembering!

Today, Arkansas is changing. But the people aren't rushing to forget their past. That's one of the things which makes Arkansas such an attractive state to visit.

Facing page: Catfish Hors d'Oeuvre.

CATFISH HORS D'OEUVRE

These well spiced and crispy morsels are a favorite in the Governor's Mansion.

Preparation Time: 20 minutes
Cooking Time: 10−15 minutes
Serves: 4−8

INGREDIENTS

4 catfish fillets, diced
1 cup yellow cornmeal
½ tsp garlic salt
½ tsp cayenne
Oil for deep fat frying

METHOD

Combine the cornmeal, garlic salt and cayenne pepper. Roll the diced catfish in this mixture to coat. Deep fry in fat which has been heated to 375°F, or until a 1-inch cube of bread browns in 1 minute. The fish pieces will sink to the bottom of the pan. When they rise to the surface they are done. The pieces should be golden brown. Drain on paper towels and serve hot.

LIZA, GOVERNOR'S MANSION,
LITTLE ROCK, AR

Facing page: Stained Glass Windows. Above: Peppered Ham.

PEPPERED HAM

This is the method used by Liza to prepare the hams which grace the table at the Governor's Mansion in Little Rock.

Preparation Time: 15 minutes
Cooking Time: 3½-4 hours
Serves: 8-10

INGREDIENTS

1 fully cooked or cured ham
Liquid Smoke
Sorghum molasses
Coarse ground pepper

METHOD

Trim the excess fat off the ham and rub it with Liquid Smoke and sorghum molasses. Sprinkle generously with coarse ground pepper to cover. Wrap the ham in aluminum foil and refrigerate overnight. The next day, remove the foil and place the ham in a shallow roasting pan. Bake at 325°F for 3½ to 4 hours.

LIZA, GOVERNOR'S MANSION,
LITTLE ROCK, AR

STAINED GLASS WINDOWS

These are a beautiful addition to a Christmas reception, and one of Liza's most often requested holiday treats.

Preparation Time: 20 minutes
Cooking Time: 5 minutes
Yield: 2 logs

INGREDIENTS

12oz semi-sweet chocolate chips
½ cup butter or margarine
6oz colored marshmallows
½ cup finely chopped pecans
12oz shredded coconut

METHOD

In the top of a double boiler, melt the chocolate drops. Allow to cool slightly, then stir in the marshmallows and pecans. Form the mixture into two logs and roll in the coconut. Refrigerate until firm. To serve, slice into ¼-inch-thick slices.

LIZA, GOVERNOR'S MANSION,
LITTLE ROCK, AR

CRUNCHYFROZEN PUNCH

This punch is a famous feature at Christmas Parties at the Governor's Mansion.

Preparation Time: 20 minutes
Cooking Time: 5 minutes
Serves: 50

INGREDIENTS

3 3oz packages jello, any flavor
9 cups boiling water
4 cups sugar
4 cups cold water
16oz lemon juice
2 46oz cans pineapple juice
6 quarts ginger ale

METHOD

Dissolve the jello in the boiling water. Combine the sugar with the cold water and bring it to the boil. Stir in the jello, and set aside to cool. When cool, add the lemon and pineapple juice. Mix well and freeze in a large plastic bucket covered with foil. To serve, place the frozen punch in a large punch bowl. Add the ginger ale and break up the frozen punch with a large knife as it thaws. The punch is ready to serve when it is slushy.

GOVERNOR'S MANSION,
LITTLE ROCK, AR

TROUT ALMONDINE

Use the freshest trout you can find to make this simple, yet elegant dish.

Preparation Time: 30 minutes
Cooking Time: 10 minutes
Serves: 2

INGREDIENTS

2 trout, cleaned and scaled
2 cups flour
1 tsp salt
Pinch cayenne pepper
4oz (1 stick) butter
Pinch dill
Pinch thyme
¼ cup lemon juice
2oz sliced almonds
2 tbsps white wine

METHOD

Season the flour with salt and cayenne. Roll the trout in the flour to coat. Melt the butter in a frying pan along with the dill and thyme. Sauté the trout in the butter for approximately 3 minutes, turn and continue cooking until the fish is done, about 3-4 minutes longer. When the trout is fully cooked add the lemon juice, white wine and almonds. Bring the liquid to a boil and simmer briefly. To serve, arrange the trout on a platter and pour the sauce on top.

GARY KETCHUM,
CREATIVE CULINARY SYSTEMS,
LITTLE ROCK, AR

CURRIED OKRA

Fried Okra is a popular and tasty vegetable side dish.

Preparation Time: 20 minutes
Cooking Time: 10-15 minutes
Serves: 4-6

Facing page: Crunchy Frozen Punch.

ARKANSAS

INGREDIENTS

1lb okra, trimmed and washed
1½ cups cornmeal
1 tsp salt
¼ tsp cayenne pepper
Oil for frying

METHOD

Wash and trim the okra, but do not dry. Combine the cornmeal and the seasonings. Roll the okra in the cornmeal until well coated. Fry in hot oil in a skillet until golden brown. Drain the okra on paper towels before serving.

GARY KETCHUM,
CREATIVE CULINARY SYSTEMS,
LITTLE ROCK, AR

RASPBERRY ICE CREAM

Here is a way to make delicious home-made ice cream without a special ice cream freezer.

Preparation Time: 20 minutes
Freezing Time: approximately 3 hours
Yield: approximately 1 quart

INGREDIENTS

2 cups sweetened condensed milk
½ cup water
4 cups fresh raspberries
4 tbsps lemon juice
1 cup heavy cream

METHOD

Combine the condensed milk, water, raspberries and lemon juice and refrigerate. Meanwhile, whip the cream in a chilled bowl until it holds a soft peak. Be careful not to overwhip and make the cream too stiff. Fold the whipped cream into the chilled raspberry mixture. Pour into a large, shallow pan and place in a very cold freezer. Freeze until half frozen, about 1½ hours, then remove. Scrape the sides and bottom of the

Trout Almondine (left) and Curried Okra (right).

pan and beat the mixture until it is smooth. Return to the freezer and freeze until firm, about 2 hours or more. Store at a normal freezer temperature.

GARY KETCHUM,
CREATIVE CULINARY SYSTEMS,
LITTLE ROCK, AR

BANANA PUDDING

This rich and creamy banana pudding is easily made and will be very much enjoyed.

Preparation Time: 10 minutes
Cooking Time: 15 minutes
Serves: 4

INGREDIENTS

2 bananas, sliced
½ cup sugar
3 tbsps cornstarch
¼ tsp salt
1 pint milk
1 tsp vanilla
1 tsp butter

METHOD

Heat the milk and add the sliced bananas. Sift together the sugar, cornstarch and salt. Stir in some of the hot milk to make a smooth paste, then stir the paste into the rest of the milk. Cook over a low heat, stirring constantly until thickened. Finally, blend in the vanilla and butter. Pour into 4 dessert glasses and chill before serving.

GARY KETCHUM,
CREATIVE CULINARY SYSTEMS,
LITTLE ROCK, AR

BLUEBERRY MUFFINS

These fresh blueberry muffins are light and delicious.

Preparation Time: 15 minutes
Cooking Time: 25 minutes
Yield: approximately 2 dozen

INGREDIENTS

2 cups flour
4 tsps baking powder
⅓ cup sugar
4 tsps baking powder
½ tsp salt
1 cup fresh blueberries, washed and drained
1 egg, beaten
¼ cup margarine, melted
1 cup milk

METHOD

Sift together the dry ingredients and stir in the blueberries. Mix together the melted margarine, egg and milk. Stir this liquid mixture into the dry ingredients and mix just enough to moisten. Fill well greased muffin pans ¾ full. Bake at 400°F for 25 minutes, or until done.

GARY KETCHUM,
CREATIVE CULINARY SYSTEMS,
LITTLE ROCK, AR

STRAWBERRY SHORTCAKE

Strawberry shortcake is a sure sign of summer, certain to bring back happy memories.

Preparation Time: 45 minutes
Cooking Time: 20 minutes
Yield: 1 large cake

INGREDIENTS

2 cups flour
3 tsps baking powder
1 tbsp sugar
¼ tsp salt
½ cup shortening
⅔ cup milk
1 egg, beaten

TOPPING

½ cup heavy cream
1 tsp confectioners' sugar
½ tsp vanilla
1 quart fresh strawberries
¼ cup sugar

Above: Blueberry Muffins (left), Banana Pudding (top center), Raspberry Ice Cream (bottom center) and Strawberry Shortcake (right).

METHOD

To mix the shortcake, sift together the dry ingredients, then cut in the shortening. Stir in the milk and eggs. Knead the dough lightly and divide into two parts. Shape to fill a well greased 9-inch round baking tin. Bake at 425°F for 20 minutes. Set aside the cake to cool while you prepare the topping. To make the topping, whip the cream and fold in the vanilla and confectioners' sugar. Set aside 5 large, well-shaped strawberries to decorate the top of the shortcake. Crush the remaining berries with the granulated sugar.

To assemble the shortcake, cut the layer in half. Spread half of the crushed strawberries on the lower half. Top with half of the whipped cream and place the upper half of the cake on top. Decorate the top of the shortcake with the reserved strawberries.

GARY KETCHUM,
CREATIVE CULINARY SYSTEMS,
LITTLE ROCK, AR

INDEX

ACKNOWLEDGMENTS

Few Europeans can properly comprehend the vastness of the America's southern states unless acquainted with the fact that they embrace an area almost as large as the whole of Europe itself. Only after our research and photographic assignment to the South for this exciting and colorful book did we realize how small our own individual European countries are. Fortunately, that realization dawned after, not before, the event. Had it been otherwise, we might have needed a good stiff drink before setting off!

Early conversations that our photographer, Jean-Paul Paireault, and I had with various Southern cooking experts seemed at times repetitive, since many traditional dishes – corn bread, corn puddings, corn muffins, and so on – kept reappearing in several states. But it was not long before we discovered that not only do traditional dishes vary in preparation from state to state, but also that there is a great deal more to Southern cooking than the old homespun recipes.

What also surprised us was the intensity of heat and humidity in those ten weeks between mid May and the end of July. Though we were soon facing problems with outdoor food photography because of the tremendous heat, the unstinting kindness and cooperation of the many people involved in the project helped to see it through. And if we were a few pounds lighter by the end of it all, it was a reflection on the weather, not the food!

Of course, our main aim was to show Southern cooking at its best, but we also wanted to combine the illustrations of the many appetizing recipes in this book with some of the stunning indoor and outdoor locations that typify the good life in the South. In these beautiful settings we believe we have captured the quintessential splendor of mansions, historic houses, and superb private residences, in all of which we were effusively welcomed and made to feel truly at home.

In venturing to say that the result is something of which everybody who was involved with us in this enormous undertaking can be proud, I would personally like to take this opportunity to thank everyone we worked with through our journey, whose willing assistance and courtesy proved that Southern hospitality is not only alive and well, but also a delight to experience.

I would also like to record a very special "thank you" to Elizabeth Lisboa-Farrow of Lisboa Associates, Inc. for the unrestricted use of her Washington, D.C. office facilities for the two weeks during which this hectic, but very enjoyable, project was being planned.

ALABAMA
Locations: The First White House of the Confederacy, Montgomery, and Sturdivant Hall, Selma

Recipes: Prepared by Creative Caterers, Montgomery from the *Once in a Blue Moon Cookbook*, Montgomery – Cecil L. McMillan 1979

Mrs. John Hawkins Napier III, Sturdivant Museum Association

ARKANSAS
Locations: The Governor's Mansion – by kind permission of Governor and Mrs. Clinton
Alexander's, formerly the Packet House, Little Rock
The residence of Mr. Carl Miller, Jr.

Recipes: Prepared by Liza from the cookbook *Thirty Years at the Mansion*

Mark R Potter, Alexander's, formerly the Packet House, Little Rock

With special thanks to Jennifer Love of the Arkansas Department of Parks and Tourism

FLORIDA
Locations: The Governor's Mansion – by kind permission of Governor (now Senator) and Mrs. Graham, Tallahassee
The residence of Mr. and Mrs. Jesse Newman, Palm Beach

Recipes: Art Smith and Liz Williams, The Governor's Mansion, Tallahassee
Chef Heinz Eberhard, Libby Thompson and Sylvia Rice of Gourmet Galley, Palm Beach

ACKNOWLEDGMENTS

GEORGIA
Locations: Rabbit Hill Farm, Atlanta – by kind permission of
    Mr. and Mrs. Hugh M. Dorsey, Jr.
The Willis House, Milledgeville

Recipes: Lowcountry Barbecue – Bennett A. Brown III,
    Atlanta
Ann Dorsey – Full Service Catering, Atlanta
Saralyn Latham, The Willis House, Milledgeville

KENTUCKY
Location: Shakertown at Pleasant Hill, Harrodsburg

Recipes: Courtesy of Elizabeth C. Kremer – from the
    Trustees House Daily Fare, Pleasant Hill, Kentucky –
    Pleasant Hill Press, Harrodsburg, Kentucky, 1970 and
    1977

LOUISIANA
Locations: Oak Alley Plantation near Vacherie
Nottaway Plantation on the River Road 2
Lafitte's Landing Restaurant, Donaldsonville
The Emberas Steak House, New Orleans
The Bayview Tavern, French Settlement
At the residence of Mr. Dan Duselier, New Orleans

Recipes: Prepared by John D. Folse of Lafitte's Landing
    Restaurant, Donaldsonville

With our special thanks to Bruce Morgan and Al Godoy,
    The State of Louisiana Office of Tourism

MISSISSIPPI
Locations: Cedar Grove Estate, Vicksburg
Grey Oaks Estate, Vicksburg
Delta Point River Restaurant, Vicksburg

Recipes: Helen Marie Abraham and Carl Andre Flowers,
    Cedar Grove Estate, Vicksburg
Ann Hall, Grey Oaks Estate, Vicksburg
Chef Martin Laffey, Delta Point River Restaurant

Our special thanks to Mrs. Lenore B. Barkley, Vicksburg-
    Warren County Tourist Commission

NORTH CAROLINA
Locations: The Fearrington House, Chapel Hill, nr. Raleigh

Recipes: Ben and Karen Barker, The Fearrington House
    Madeleine Kamman's *In Madeleine's Kitchen*
Walter Royal and *Maida Heatter's Book of Great Chocolate
    Desserts*

SOUTH CAROLINA
Location: Residence of Mr. and Mrs. Roger P. Hanahan
Residence of Mr. Richard Jenrette
The gardens of Magnolia Plantation
The gardens of Drayton Hall

Recipes: Prepared by Lucille J. Grant from *Charleston
    Receipts,* compiled and edited by the Junior League of
    Charleston, Inc.

Flowers and food styling: José Vilela, New York City

TENNESSEE
Locations: Centennial Park, Parthenon Building, Nashville
The Dixon Gallery and Gardens, Memphis

Recipes: Prepared and styled by CF Marketing Associates,
    Nashville
Mrs. Doris Belcher, Memphis
Ann Cox, Murfreesboro
Mary Ann Fowlkes, Nashville
Callie Lillie Owen – Courtesy of Nashville Cookbook
Pat Coker, Nashville
Mary Stanfill – courtesy of Nashville Cookbook
Courtesy Jack Daniel's Distillery, Lynchburg
Elsie Walker, Springfield
Cream Cheese Pound Cake recipe from *The Southern
    Heritage Cakes Cookbook*, 1983 reproduced by kind
    permission of Oxmoor House, Inc., book division of
    Southern Progress Corporation, Birmingham, AL.

VIRGINIA
Locations: Woodlawn Plantation, Mount Vernon
The Ships Cabin Seafood Restaurant, Norfolk
Phillips Waterside, Norfolk

Recipes: Prepared by Ridgewells Caterer, Inc.
Taken from *The Woodlawn Plantation Cook Book* edited by
    Joan Smith
Original recipes from Woodlawn Plantation, Mount Vernon
    – Nicole Sours, Director
Joe Hoggard and Susan Painter, The Ships Cabin Seafood
    Restaurant
Brice and Shirley Phillips of Phillips Waterside, Norfolk

Our special thanks to Diann Stutz, the Norfolk Convention
    and Visitors Bureau,

Hanni Penrose